SUCCESSFUL PUBLIC MEETINGS

A Practical Guide

ELAINE COGAN

PLANNERS BOOK SERVICE
AMERICAN PLANNING ASSOCIATION
Chicago, Illinois
Washington D.C.

This second edition is rededicated
with love to my husband Arnold.
If everyone conducted public meetings as well as you
do, there would be no need for this book.

Second edition

Copyright © 2000 by the American Planning Association,
122 S. Michigan Ave., Suite 1600, Chicago, IL 60603-6107

ISBN (paperback) 1-884829-38-4
ISBN (hardbound) 1-884829-39-2
Library of Congress Catalog Card Number: 99-75581

The first edition of this book was copyrighted in 1992 by Jossey-Bass Inc.

Photo credits:
Front cover: Top left, Elaine Cogan; other photos, Toni Wise
Back cover: Bruce Luzader

Contents

Preface

This book began as a gleam in the eye of my first publisher, who called me one day to say, "I've heard of your workshops on how to hold effective meetings. There doesn't seem to be anything definitive published on that subject. How would you like to write a book?"

His query started me thinking about what I have come to realize is the art and science of designing and managing these ubiquitous events. Most of us have been in meetings when citizens became hostile after being treated in a demeaning or condescending manner. We have tried to stay awake as panel discussions dragged on way beyond their time limit. We have suffered through audiovisual presentations that were too long or impossible to read. We probably also have witnessed, or even participated in, some outstanding public meetings—meetings at which everything seemed to work out. A successful meeting is the reward for studious attention to many factors; it is not the result of luck or happenstance.

As a writer and consultant in communications, I have been working for more than 25 years to design and facilitate public meetings that produce the desired results, both for my clients and for the public.

There is considerable literature about components of successful meetings, such as techniques for facilitating discussion or for reaching agreement in difficult or contentious situations. Each method has its adherents and some record of success, but each is just as likely to fail in the wrong context or environment. I am pleased to present this ready reference that addresses the totality of factors, the host of minor and major details that stand between success and failure. When read from beginning to end, this book provides a full accounting of everything needed to hold a successful public meeting. Those who want specific information on matters such as how to work with the media or facilitate a discussion can turn to a particular chapter.

To produce this second edition, I have re-read every word,

updating where needed; for example, adding information about e-mail and web sites not even thought of when the first book was written. I also have added a final chapter in question and answer form that covers the common themes that seem to concern most meeting planners at my workshops and seminars.

It is with sincere gratitude that I acknowledge Sylvia Lewis, Director of Publications for the American Planning Association, my editor and mentor for this edition. Sylvia's belief in the value of this subject and her nurturing of the publication enables this book to reach even more people who engage in this timeless American ritual of holding public meetings.

Organization

Chapter 1 of this book rightly concerns leadership, the most important factor in ensuring the success of any public meeting. Managers can motivate staff people to do a superior job only if they themselves understand the importance of attending to all the details and participate at key times during the process. They must transmit this understanding to their staffs in words and deeds, delegate responsibility appropriately, and allocate all the necessary resources.

Leadership is a prime ingredient of success at the meeting itself, as descriptions of the distinct roles and qualifications of the chairperson, facilitator, discussion leader, and recorder attest. The planners of the public meeting should be candid when assigning various leadership roles and consider the ability of each participant. If, for example, the mayor or company president must be the convener but lacks the skills of a good facilitator, a more qualified person should take on the latter role while the status of Mr. or Ms. In Charge is maintained.

Chapter 2, Different Types of Public Meetings, makes the point that no single meeting format can serve all purposes; thus, at the outset of planning, it is important that organizers decide on the meeting's primary goal. They need to define the purpose fully, so that all that follows—the material sent to the public, the structure and format of the presentations and discussion, and the follow-up—is appropriate to advancing the meeting's aims. Certainty and consistency are major factors in gaining and keeping public trust and acceptance.

Chapters 3 and 4 explain details that are essential to the success of any public meeting, yet too many meeting planners ignore: effective ways first to notify the public and then create a comfortable environment once people are there. The importance of promising only as much as one can deliver and providing an atmosphere conducive to reaching the articulated goals cannot be overly stressed. Readers will have greater empathy for international negotiators who haggle over the shape of the conference table when they realize the effect of such details on the successful outcome of their meetings.

Dedicating adequate time for planning the meeting is a continual message in this book, and this certainly includes the actual presentations of staff and others. Though rank in the organization is frequently a factor in choosing who speaks when, it should not be the only consideration. Knowledge of the subject is important, of course, but so is the ability to present information clearly and succinctly to laypeople. Because that ability is rarely innate, numerous useful techniques are explained in Chapter 5.

With the advent of computers that can produce complex graphic displays, too many novices believe they can be instant artists. Instead, most amateurs turn out mediocre charts, graphs, and other materials. They can do more audiovisuals in less time, but not necessarily better ones. Audiovisual aids of any type must be part of the overall planning for the meeting so that appropriate techniques are chosen, and they must be executed carefully so that they advance the audience's understanding of the subject. For easy reference, much of Chapter 6 is presented in chart form that summarizes advantages, disadvantages, and usage guidelines for each audiovisual technique.

Apathetics, hair-splitters, know-it-alls, sneak-outers: these and many other types of people likely to be encountered at a public meeting are described in detail in Chapter 7. Chairpeople and facilitators must always treat each participant with respect, but they also must be firm in advancing the aims of the meeting and guarding the rights of the majority.

The media are another audience with whom meeting planners must contend. Chapter 8 shows how understanding the differing objectives and requirements of the press, radio, and television can help meeting planners obtain more fair and adequate coverage. What to do when the media err and how and to whom to address complaints also are discussed.

Chapter 9 contains a definitive checklist for meeting planners, and covers everything that needs to be done before, during, and after the public meeting. The only shortcut to success is the experience garnered by using techniques that work.

Throughout the book, the reader will find examples that illustrate specific ideas or concepts. As bizarre as some of the stories may seem, they are all real; each one happened sometime—most often to hapless meeting planners, sometimes to the author, who should have known better.

The last, and new, chapter is a summary of the questions most frequently asked at my seminars and workshops.

At this crucial time in the life of our democratic society, when the public is more vocal than ever before about playing an active role in public policy, those who plan and hold public meetings cannot be ill-informed or cavalier. As you learn how to do it, I hope you also will have fun in the doing!

Elaine Cogan
Portland, Oregon
December 1999

About the Author

Elaine Cogan is a partner in the Portland, Oregon, planning and communications consulting firm of Cogan Owens Cogan. She has designed and facilitated hundreds of public meetings: from the 1960s when she calmed down gun-waving activists who threatened a few dozen participants at neighborhood meetings, through the 1970s and '80s when she involved thousands of citizens in 26 communities to help solve the problems of financing public elementary and secondary education; and in the last decade of the 20th century, when the citizen involvement program she designed for Portland's Future Focus strategic planning process received an "Outstanding Achievement" award from the U.S. Conference of Mayors. The League of Women Voters of Oregon recognized her as an "Outstanding Woman of Achievement" who believes in and practices a philosophy for public meetings that minimizes confrontation, encourages all participants to air their views, and produces a reasonable and supportable consensus.

As a consultant to the burgeoning Oregon communities of Gresham, Hood River and Medford, Cogan developed and facilitated vision projects to guide each community's future growth and development. A unique component of each process involved the youth of the city who produced hundreds of essays, poems, and drawings that were taken into account by adult decision makers. In other communities such as Anchorage, Alaska, Cogan designed and facilitated similar vision projects that excited and engaged the imaginations and talents of a broad cross-section of citizens. She is highly respected for her innovative approaches and abilities to facilitate difficult meetings.

Cogan is the co-author, with the late Ben Padrow, of *You Can Talk to (Almost) Anyone about (Almost) Anything: A Speaking Guide for Business and Professional People,* and is an adviser and consultant throughout the United States. She has been an editorial columnist for the *Oregon Journal* and the *Oregonian* newspapers, producer/moderator of a radio talk show, and is a television commentator on public issues. She is a member of the national academic honor societies Phi Kappa Phi and Omicron Nu.

A native of Brooklyn, New York, Cogan has lived in Portland, Oregon, for many years with her husband and business partner, Arnold, three grown children, and six grandchildren.

Introduction

When You Have to Face the Public

Many executives or managers cringe at the very idea of holding or participating in a public meeting, and for good reason! Public meetings are unpredictable. They are messy. They often become arenas where people confront each other passionately on issues. They can be time consuming to organize and tedious to attend, taking precious time away from getting on with the matter at hand and reaching a solution.

Given the generally unsatisfactory nature of many public meetings, it is no wonder that many people responsible for them face the prospect with the same dread they feel when they go to the dentist: They may have to do it, but they do not have to like it. But, while the dentist is prepared for and able to handle unwilling patients, too many meeting managers are ill prepared or even hostile to the prospect of dealing with the public. On their side, citizens can become cranky or even downright obstreperous if they are subjected to meetings that do not meet their expectations. That does not mean they must have their needs or demands met entirely. The public does, however, expect and deserve to be treated honestly, fairly, and with respect.

Despite our resistance or aversion, there are many compelling reasons to hold a meeting with the public. For political jurisdictions, the most prevalent is administrative or legal: They are required as part of the process of informing and obtaining the approval of their constituencies. For example, the federal government must hold hearings to give the public the opportunity to comment on matters such as highway projects and food and drug policies, and most local and state governments have similar requirements. But even the most regimented and formal public hearings can be made innovative and interesting, as we will see in further chapters.

Another reason to hold a public meeting is strategic, particularly for private or nonprofit organizations who may be dealing with public issues. Even when you are not required to invite the public into the deliberations, it may be a very good idea if you do. Enlisting the public as a partner, or at the least, informing it of your point of view, can defuse potential opposition, acquire allies in unlikely places, and unite a community and its leaders around a common purpose. It also builds trust. The process of holding an effective public meeting itself can be a product. When people carry away good feelings and positive attitudes, they have confidence in the sponsor that can be a cornerstone for trust in other projects and programs.

> *For 90 years, the private local electric utility company owned and operated a dam for electrical generation in a pristine wilderness 30 miles from a dense urban area. A by-product of the dam was a lake the company had built and maintained for public use. Thousands of people were accustomed to enjoying it for boating, swimming, and picnicking and the public had full expectations it would always remain "theirs." Shortly before the summer season, the company was sold to a mega-conglomerate that announced its intention to breach the dam because it was no longer a cost-effective generator of electricity. Additionally, the company said this action would aid the survival of salmon, an endangered species under federal law. However, without the dam, the river would flow free and the lake would disappear.*
>
> *The public first became aware of the company's intentions through an article in the local newspaper. Though this was an action well within the company's right to take, the news caused a public outcry, not only from nearby rural neighbors, but from city dwellers many miles away who had been accustomed to enjoying this beautiful outdoor area. After many angry letters and phone calls, the company finally agreed to hold a public meeting, although officials insisted the corporate decision would not be changed.*
>
> *At the meeting, the small rural school cafeteria overflowed with frustrated citizens facing stony-faced corpo-*

> *rate spokespeople. While some people questioned the*
> *"right" of the company to close down the dam, several*
> *others pleaded for a phasing in of the decision, "one more*
> *year" to enjoy "their" lake. However, company spokes-*
> *people said they were not authorized to compromise.*
>
> *As the grumbling citizenry filed out, dissatisfied and*
> *disgusted, several people were already organizing to*
> *protest the company's request for a rate increase at the*
> *next meeting of the State Public Utilities Commission.*
> *The company may have won the battle of the lake, but it*
> *faced losing a far more important war: public acceptance*
> *on matters essential to its financial future.*

There are many lessons that can be learned from this true incident. First, we can question whether the company should have
exposed itself to the public in a forum in which it was sure to be the
loser. It had lost credibility previously in failing to gauge the depth
of the public's affection for "their" lake by announcing closure as if
it were only a corporate concern. Furthermore, company spokespeople at the meeting were not authorized to compromise with the
public in any way, and thus were exposed to negative remarks and
insults to which they could not respond with anything positive. The
damage from this ill-conceived and poorly managed public meeting
will haunt the company for years to come. It might have been more
productive for all if, earlier in its decision-making process, the utility had sought out small groups of influential or concerned people
in the community or elsewhere who favored protecting the salmon,
so that the company's position was not portrayed as only self-serv-
ing. It also would have helped matters if utility spokespeople had
been allowed to show some good will by being flexible in how or
when it closed the lake.

In the above case, the wrong type of meeting was held to address
a specific problem, and the resulting disaster was predictable. It is
folly to expect one format to fit all situations. Moreover, success
does not come without hard work, and adequate time and resources
must be allocated to carry out each important detail. On the other
hand, just one major success can make believers of even the most
cynical individuals.

What, then, are measurements of success? How can we tell when
we have had a constructive and effective public meeting? The most

immediate and accurate indicator is our own feeling when it is over. We may be tired, even exhausted; we may wish we had answered a particular question differently or chosen a more suitable chart or graph. But if we know overall that the meeting was productive and interesting and that the audience participated in a positive manner, we can feel satisfied.

None of this just happens, however; a successful public meeting is the result of a three-part process: pre-meeting planning, careful execution, and honest debriefing.

Planning is essential. Success is highly unlikely if you treat the meeting as an add-on to an already overburdened schedule, accept any available location without checking it out beforehand, ask any staff people who happen to be free to make the presentations, and/or get to the room just in time, with no idea whether you will face an audience of 20 or 200. In other words, if you have a cavalier attitude toward the public meeting, you court disaster. We laugh when we read of diplomats who spend weeks arguing over room size and the configuration of tables and chairs before they settle down to discuss weighty international issues, but we would sympathize if we realized how crucial these factors are to our own success.

In planning your public meeting, the first question to ask is: Why are we having it? Managers and their top assistants, as well as any staff members who are actively involved in the issue, should get together for an honest assessment. The format and structure should be developed only after you have ascertained the reason for the meeting. Ask yourselves: What public purpose will be served? Informational? Advisory? Decision making? A combination? If the decision, such as the lake matter illustrated above, has already been made behind closed doors and the best you can hope for is little or no public outcry, it may be better not to hold a general meeting at all.

If you have decided that there are sufficient reasons to hold a public meeting, choose the team that will be responsible for the event and divide up responsibilities. Team leaders should not necessarily be the technical people who have the best data or information on the subject under discussion. In fact, technicians often do not possess the appropriate meeting-organizational skills. Technical experts are good in their places: to present data or complicated information. But they must be kept to strict time limits and not allowed to drone on and on without proper visual aids and the assistance of people who speak a language the audience understands. An effective public meeting agenda has room for the experts but also assigns clear roles to all the participants. Your team should consist of at least the following:

- Director, to lead the way in setting overall goals and objectives and to make decisions on policy issues.
- Meeting manager, skilled in group dynamics and able to deal with all the important factors that make a meeting a success.
- Unflappable assistant in charge of such details as finding a suitable location, notification, name tags, food, handouts, and keeping up-to-date on all problems.
- Media liaison who understands the requirements of the press, radio, and television.
- Chair, facilitator, discussion leaders, technical presenters, recorders, and others as the format requires.
- One or more people who understand the project or the process and can bring a needed technical, political, historical, or other necessary perspective.
- Experts in presentation and audiovisual techniques.

The team should have its initial meeting at least six weeks before the event and draw up a detailed schedule of activities, including deadlines and responsibilities.

There often are minimum legal requirements that underlie notification procedures for public meetings; for example, having to apprise all property owners within a certain distance of a proposed local development. But the savvy meeting planner reaches out further. However, even if you use an extensive and up-to-date list, few people may be motivated to attend your meeting if your notice is reader-unfriendly. Many official notices are so packed with legalese and jargon that citizens take one glance and throw them away in confusion or disgust, only to find out too late that a public matter has been approved against their wishes. The public official may retort defensively, "Where were you when we asked for public comment? We sent you a notice," but this may not be enough to mollify angry citizens. They may mount recall campaigns, take legal action, or find other ways to redress their feelings of betrayal. Public agencies certainly must follow the proscribed requirements for notice, but in many cases, they should take further steps to reach people who may be concerned.

Private companies or nonprofit organizations that do not operate under public notification laws have more latitude to be creative in their notices. Ads in local newspapers, direct mail, telephone calls, and publicity through other organizations are just some ways to get the word out.

To adapt an architectural expression, the format of a meeting should always follow its function. If past public meetings have always been done a certain way, but the reason is lost in antiquity and the meetings are marginally effective anyway, have the courage at least to be willing to consider other structures.

You must, however, have a context. Before you choose your format, identify the needs of your audience. Wise meeting planners avoid the pitfall of having only one approach or process that they trot out for all occasions. Recognize, too, that few people are multi-purpose presenters, appropriate for all occasions. Some relate very well at neighborhood shirt-sleeve meetings but freeze with fright if they have to make formal presentations to large groups. Others enjoy the on-stage aspects of the latter and hate to meet people eye-to-eye. Only after a careful analysis of your audience should you choose the appropriate program, process, and participants.

I hope this book will inspire readers to cut loose from the déjà vu school of meeting planning, even if one process has worked (or at least kept you and your organization out of serious trouble) the last 255 times. While the primary reason to consider other ways of doing things is to gain more productive public participation and acceptance, an important byproduct is to motivate public meeting planners. Conscientious executives appreciate the team-building aspects of this approach. As staff people work together intensively on a successful public meeting, they develop a communal spirit and a respect for each other that can carry into other aspects of work.

Good planning only gets you to the starting line, however. Lack of attention to effective presentations, an uncertain or dogmatic chair, facilitators and discussion leaders who ignore carefully developed schedules and agendas, inept audiovisuals, and general sloppiness counteract the most meticulous pre-meeting efforts.

As discussed in later chapters, there are many ways to involve and give people a sense of ownership in the process and the results. It is important to choose the right process for each particular subject, time, and place, and to create and maintain an environment that enables people to work together to discuss difficult issues or solve problems, an environment in which they feel safe and comfortable.

In addition to willingly committing leadership, their own time, and staff resources to planning and carrying out public meetings, managers and executives can make another important contribution to success by exuding a sense of excitement and anticipation. As you develop meeting organizational skills, you will begin to enjoy those previously dreaded events and communicate your positive feelings to your staff as well as to the audience.

As tired as you all may be after the public meeting, do not neglect the postmeeting debriefing. If everyone is willing after you have packed up, go out for coffee, dessert, or a pizza with all the staff participants and perhaps some friendly onlookers, or schedule a half-hour or so the next day for a recap. While the details are still fresh in everyone's mind, be candid. What worked? What did not? Could everyone see and understand the audiovisuals? Are there ways you could have defused those hostile questions with more ease? Did the right people make the presentations? Did Frank's stage fright show too much and cause him too much anxiety? (Maybe he is better behind the scenes and would be relieved to have someone else make the presentation next time.) Learn from your mistakes and applaud your successes.

For more specific guidelines, read on!

1

Leadership: The Key To Successful Public Meetings

The single most important ingredient in assuring the success of a public meeting is clear and decisive leadership. Every factor described in this book—correct format, receiver-friendly notice, appropriate environment, clear presentations, positive media relationships, and all the rest—is an additional essential element in helping you have a successful public meeting. But citizens will endure all manner of inconvenience and forgive those inevitable glitches if they believe in their leaders. Conversely, the most ideal setting and circumstances cannot make up for inadequate leadership. The audience gives meeting sponsors and presenters a precious possession: its time. A good leader appreciates that gift and uses it wisely. Managers or executives can and should delegate many aspects of organizing and running meetings, but they need to realize that they alone set the scene for success or failure.

Effective leaders understand the dynamic tension between content and context, between what is communicated and how it is communicated. It is easier to find the experts to provide data and information than to design the process that will enable people to work together in a positive environment to discuss difficult issues or solve problems. As noted in Chapter 2, which explores types of public meetings, there are many ways to deal with the same issue. Leaders need to work with staff members to find the right process for each particular time, place, audience, and subject.

There are two common leadership roles at public meetings: the chairperson and the facilitator. As the highest ranking individual at the meeting, the chair is responsible for representing the sponsor and presiding over the agenda, particularly the beginning and ending. The chair greets and introduces people and sets the general tone. The facilitator then assumes the task of making it all happen as planned and directing the flow of information and discussion. Recorders, discussion leaders, resource people, and others take their cues from the facilitator, though they may be introduced by the chair. While in some cases one individual can take both roles, usually it is advisable to divide up these duties.

ATTRIBUTES OF LEADERSHIP

Both the chairperson and the facilitator must be conversant with the subjects under discussion. While they leave the details to others, they should know enough about the issues to recognize when the discussion is getting off the track and/or when disrupters promulgate false or misleading information.

Leaders also must be fair at all times and be able to leave any strong personal opinions behind as they mount the podium. They may have to be firm in keeping to the agenda and schedule, but always within a context that treats all citizens equitably and with goodwill.

In a democracy, true leadership comes by minimizing, not accentuating, the trappings of power. The presidential seal travels wherever the President of the United States goes and is placed on the podium before he/she speaks; but his ability to lead does not come from his official title. Some dignitaries flaunt flags, banners, assistants, and sycophants as evidence of their importance. Others create a distance between themselves and the public by standing on a raised stage or dais. These devices often backfire and alienate citizens from their leaders if there is no substance to back them up. If the public does not believe it is being treated with respect, it will find a way to fight back, whether by disrupting the proceedings, taking to the streets before or after, voting nay on specific issues at the ballot box, or not voting at all, turning the "rascals" out of office, or resorting to the courts.

Effective leaders know how to maintain the proper balance between formality and informality. Many times, those who rule exclusively by the book hide behind an unreasonably strict structure that discourages citizen participation and interaction because they are afraid that the meeting will get out of their control. They use time as a weapon: Having allowed their chosen experts to monopolize the agenda, they then claim that there is not enough time to give the public a chance to speak. They run the meeting solely in the interest of their organization or themselves.

At the other extreme, casual, laid-back, anything-goes leaders may make the public feel good at the time because there was such a free-flowing discussion. But savvy people often feel betrayed and manipulated after the euphoria wears off when they realize it was all for show and nothing lasting was accomplished.

Leaders who have energy and enthusiasm, who are upbeat and positive, are forgiven many other faults. People want to follow leaders whose sense of excitement is revealed by their words and deeds. On the other hand, leaders with low energy convey apathy and disinterest. Their attributes are also contagious, but in a negative way.

Effective leaders use praise unsparingly. They do not hesitate to compliment individuals without necessarily passing judgment on the content of their remarks. "Jesse, we certainly appreciate your reminding us of the history of our neighborhood. It puts an interesting perspective on the issues we're talking about tonight." It is not necessary for the leader to indicate whether she likes or dislikes Jesse's "perspective." It is more important that she praises the old-timer for being willing to make a contribution to the discussion and thus ensures his continued participation.

THE CHAIRPERSON

Executives, managers, directors, mayors, or other acknowledged leaders are the most logical choice to chair public meetings. They should participate in planning by helping to decide the broad objectives and general process of the meeting and then take part in the dress rehearsal, while delegating the details of the preplanning to subordinates. Details of the meeting itself also should be delegated. If the projector light burns out or the microphone is having feedback problems, others should have been assigned to take care of them. The chair has enough to do being the host, greeting people, and making everyone feel comfortable. This host function is especially important if the subject of the meeting is controversial or if some attendees are expected to be contentious or antagonistic. The most effective technique for disarming the opposition is to stand at the door as people come in, smile at friend and foe alike, greet them by name (if you know it), and extend an open hand. The most effective way to feed the opposition's paranoia and destructive tendencies and ensure that antagonists will try to obstruct the process is to turn away when you see them coming or be too busy with housekeeping details to give them respect.

If at all possible, the chair should be introduced to the media before the meeting. Someone else should be charged with inviting the media to the event, finding them and bringing them over, but the chair should be the primary person available for interviews and comments. On the other hand, the chair should not delay starting the meeting on time because of a lengthy media interview. Instead, he or she should agree to be available at the first opportunity to continue the interview—perhaps after opening the meeting or during the break.

The chair sets the tone for a well-ordered meeting by beginning and ending on time. Any delay in starting should be for a very good reason. Sparse attendance is not one of them, as the expected number of people may never show up. Moreover, by beginning within five minutes of the scheduled time, the chair respects those who followed the rules and shows latecomers that they missed something by being tardy. In the opening remarks, the chair can make everyone feel welcome and at ease by following this order:

Never assume that everyone knows who you are. Introduce yourself: "Good evening, I'm glad to see so many familiar faces. I hope that by the end of the meeting we'll all get to know each other. I'm Jenny Goodman, your city planning director and chair of this evening's meeting." Continue by saying something personal that begins to build a bridge to your audience: "I've been in Plainview for five years, and one of the best parts of my work is meeting with citizens such as yourselves." Or, if Goodman is new to the community, she might add this personal note: "I've only been here a few months, but already, you've made me feel at home." In both cases, she could add, "It makes my job easier when citizens such as yourselves care to spend time talking about the important issues that are on tonight's agenda." Note the friendly neutrality of her remarks. She indicates her loyalty to the community and compliments the citizens for participating, without prejudging what they might want to say.

Next, review the purpose, agenda, and ground rules of the meeting. If this is a formal event and you are taking testimony only from people who have registered beforehand, say so. If at all possible, have a system for receiving written remarks. Tell people how their testimony or comments will be used in the decision-making process, and when the decisions will be made. If there will be time for general discussion or small-group breakouts, tell participants when that will be. People want certainty and respect just as much as they want involvement. They will honor any reasonable agenda, if they are told beforehand what it is in a manner that assures them that everyone will be treated fairly.

It is important also to explain the logistics, particularly the location of the restrooms and microphones, and when and where any refreshments may be available. Let the audience know of restrictions on parking that may cause offending cars to be towed.

Every community has political or other celebrities. If they are attending the meeting, introduce them after making sure your assistant has written down all their names and titles phonetically so you can pronounce them correctly. Have some idea where they are sitting so that you can look generally in their direction. Do not invite them to speak unless it is a strategic necessity. If you fear they will give a speech instead of a few perfunctory remarks, review the agenda for all to hear, subtly showing they are an "add on" and it is time to move on. Discourage all applause, even at the end. This is a serious public meeting, not a performance or rally. If there are people you need to acknowledge who are not there, save them for last: "Having introduced our mayor and the chief of police, I now want to mention that the regional welfare supervisor had a last-minute change of schedule that kept him away. He told me to be sure to give you his warm greetings and said he was anxious to read all your comments."

After these preliminaries, introduce the facilitator, who then · takes over the meeting and introduces others, such as resource people or discussion leaders. Then retire unobtrusively from the front of the room instead of standing or sitting within view. It is important that the chair be inconspicuous until the end of the meeting and not disrupt the proceedings by holding court in a corner with a few cronies or favorite citizens. This is an opportune time to be interviewed by the media, but only if you find a corridor or another room away from the primary action. Some chairpeople, truly having no part to play in the proceedings, leave the premises and return near the end. This is acceptable if they leave quietly and come back in enough time to be briefed on anything unexpected that may have occurred in their absence. In a potentially volatile situation, however, it is smarter for chairpeople to remain nearby to be ready to make any necessary, last-minute executive decisions. Moreover, by listening quietly, the chair can observe what the busy staff members may overlook. It is important, however, that the chair not seem to diminish or call into question the authority of the facilitator or others who have been given the responsibility of running the meeting.

The chair takes center stage before the end of the meeting only when a problem such as a demonstration or disruption calls for a higher authority. How the chair makes an unscheduled appearance is a matter of preference and ability. Neutral, highly regarded chairpeople who have had no part in the heated proceedings may deal well with conflicts and field hostile questions diplomatically, while more partisan chairpeople may appear only to fan the flames. If they can maintain a neutral demeanor, chairpeople can speak for the policy of the organization with more certainty than either the facilitator or the resource people.

The chair's concluding summary should include a short overview of what occurred at the meeting and what will happen next. Is this the only public discussion of the issue? Will there be others? Where and when? How will the organization use or respond to the citizens' comments received at this meeting? Will the outcome of this meeting become part of a report to be given to other decision makers? Are there opportunities for further written comments? Will minutes be sent to all participants, or can people pick up a recap somewhere? What are the next steps? If the chair feels too uninformed to make a meaningful summary, the facilitator can do it, but someone must tie up all the loose ends before the meeting is over.

It is as important to have a structure for closing as it is for opening. Always end when scheduled, even if there seems to be unfinished business. When you called the meeting, you made a pact with the audience for a particular time and format, and they have every right to expect you to keep your word. Time can be an ally if the meeting is being disrupted by angry or hostile people: "I know that there are still some issues we haven't addressed, but we promised to end at 9:30 and it's 9:25. We have to wind up now, but we'll be glad to stay later to speak to you individually."

Before you make a graceful exit, thank everyone for coming and assure people how much you value their participation.

FACILITATOR AND DISCUSSION LEADER

The chair is the scene setter; the facilitator is the enabler. Discussion leaders, resource people, and all the others important to well-functioning meetings get their cues from the facilitator. The role of the facilitator is to stimulate, organize, and synthesize the thinking of the group. Many times, you hope the discussion can lead to consensus. Sometimes an agreement to disagree may be the best that can be attained, but the facilitator helps the group go as far as it can, without ridiculing, arguing, or ignoring anyone's point of view.

The most satisfying facilitation is with a group of 25 or fewer, when the facilitator can see people eye to eye and engage them individually as well as collectively. If the group numbers in the hundreds, successful facilitation is often primarily a case of fielding questions graciously from as many people as possible in the time allowed.

If genuine discussion and analysis of alternatives is desired, it is best to engage people in smaller units. Each group can then be led by a discussion leader, with the group facilitator responsible for the overall conduct of the meeting. With large groups or small, preparation, patience, and a positive attitude are attributes necessary for success.

While it is important that the group leader knows the material well enough to understand when the discussion is going off on unproductive tangents, it is not necessary to be the technical expert or guru; there should be resource people to fulfill that function. It is essential to have good listening and synthesizing skills, to be accepting of different points of view, and patient with slow thinkers or people who have difficulty expressing themselves.

Good facilitators and discussion leaders maintain a healthy balance between friendliness and firmness. Benevolence should not be construed as permission to someone who wants to dominate the meeting. The leader should use the agenda to keep the group from straying: "Yes, Mary, I can see that your idea would be a good one if we were talking about sewers, but tonight we're trying to decide how we should spend our park budget. What's your opinion about that?"

Take the pulse of the group regularly so that you do not push people into polarization or force them to make premature decisions. Aim for consensus and general areas of agreement that allow everyone to come away with something rather than a vote in which there will be clear winners and losers. Give credence to differences, but do not let them bog down the process: "We seem to disagree on that point, but I noticed everyone nodding on the other issues. Let's see, then. We have consensus on items one, two, and four."

The leader aids the group process by continually paraphrasing and synthesizing: "If we combine Jim's idea of doubling the number of benches with Florence's about adding cookstoves, are we suggesting that we want a new picnic area?" Make sure participants nod or show their agreement before you move on. Remain alert to when the group has exhausted the subject and is willing to discuss another issue. Wrap it up when it is obvious that people have nothing more to say.

Facilitators and discussion leaders must always resist the temptation to voice their own opinions and should never argue or allow others to engage in an argument: "Getting out various points of view is what this process is all about. Now that we've heard from Marie and Frank, let's go around the table and see what the rest of us have to say about this."

Effective leaders are not afraid to say that they do not know. If you are asked a technical question that requires an answer before the discussion can proceed, try to find a resource person in the room. If no one knows, or if the answer really does not make a difference in the deliberations, indicate this tactfully: "I'm sorry no one seems to know the answer to that now, but let's assume that the budget will be the same as last year. What priorities would you all suggest?"

Use various techniques to stimulate or control discussion. If things bog down, try schoolteacher style: "When you hear the words 'clean environment,' what comes to your mind?" Or direct: "What do you think of when you hear the words 'clean environment,' Jason?"

Follow-up: "Peter, I see you're nodding. What's your opinion of what Jason said?" If you have an enthusiastic group in which everyone talks at once, introduce some order: "Let's see, we're going to have to slow down if everyone is to get a chance. I think Clarence had his hand up first, then Hortense, and then Elizabeth." Or, "Everyone obviously has something to say about this. Let's go around the table, starting with Robert."

While facilitators must never disavow the democratic process, they must be willing to make procedural decisions without entertaining a long discussion: "We have an hour to discuss three topics, but the last one, funding, is more complicated, so I'm going to allot more time to it unless anyone objects."

Above all, the best facilitators and discussion leaders keep cool, calm, and in command.

For hints about how to deal with different types of participants, please refer to Chapter 7.

THE RECORDER

As noted in Chapter 2, the responsibility of the recorder is to take notes that can be read easily by all participants. Some facilitators prefer to be their own recorders, while others welcome an extra pair of eyes, ears, and hands. The role of the recorder is to show all participants that their opinions are being given credence and permanence by writing them down; provide a visible record and point of reference for all; depersonalize the discussion for future use by not attributing anyone's name to the ideas and comments; provide a sense of continuity and movement; and give newcomers the opportunity to catch up without having to interrupt the discussion.

If a verbatim transcript is required, hire trained court reporters. Otherwise, be selective when paraphrasing individual comments and the overall discussion so that they are not lost in a sea of details. The best recorders for public meetings are not stenographers trained to ignore content but astute listeners who can synthesize impartially. To assist recorders in their task, the meeting organizer should make sure that they understand the context and general language of the discussion and are attuned to the nuances of the subject, alert to the circuitous path the discussion may take.

Recorders also must be able to assimilate diverse ideas rapidly and accurately. They are the servants, not the masters, of the process and should not make a habit of holding up the discussion because they cannot keep up. Once in a while, it is acceptable to ask, "Let me see, before I write it down, I think I heard three separate points here," and then to paraphrase them. This enables the recorder and the group to catch up with each other. In general, however, recorders may very well run down before the group runs out of ideas. That is a hazard that goes with the job.

Facilitators and recorders must maintain a good working relationship. This is more easily accomplished if they agree on the ground rules ahead of time. Will the facilitators synthesize the information for the recorders, or are the latter more or less on their own? How much information will be recorded, and when? Are the recorders to be seen and not heard, or may they interrupt (within reason, of course)?

It is important to be flexible. Recorders do not "own" their information and should not be possessive about it. The written record belongs to all the discussants.

Recorders should write more, not less. Those who wait for the perfect phrase or summary may miss important points.

A sense of humor can often defuse a tense or potentially volatile situation. This trait is important to all leaders, but particularly to recorders, who may be blamed unfairly when the message that they write carries bad news.

In addition to all these admirable traits, effective meeting leaders—chairpeople, facilitators, and recorders—have a sixth sense that keeps them and their meetings out of trouble. While that sense cannot be taught explicitly, it is nurtured when attention is paid to all the other attributes discussed in the chapters that follow.

Other important roles are played by resource people, those who are expert in a particular topic or issue under discussion. They are not leaders in the meeting, and in fact, need to take care they do not take over or dominate because they think they know more than anyone else. They are essential in giving correct information at the appropriate time, but they take their cues from the chair and facilitator.

2

Different Types of Public Meetings

Regulatory and advisory boards and commissions, committees, task forces, forums, workshops, sponsored by appointed, self-appointed, or elected bodies—all public meetings take place for at least one of three general purposes: to provide information, give advice, or solve problems. As noted previously, the first matter to consider in planning any meeting is its primary objective. Then, develop the appropriate structure and organization to meet that objective.

INFORMATIONAL MEETINGS

These public meetings are held primarily to convey information or data to decision makers or interested citizens. Examples are legislative or administrative hearings, sessions of elected officials, forums sponsored by private companies or nonprofit organizations engaged in matters affecting the public, and meetings of interested people such as neighborhoods or civic organizations.

The communication at informational meetings is generally one-way, from the presenters to the audience. Although the former usually are professional staff, they also may be outside experts. Asking questions of the individuals who provide information may be allowed, but an ongoing dialogue between the presenters and the audience is likely to be discouraged. If the public is allowed to testify or present formal remarks, individuals usually are asked to sign up in advance; state their name, address, and affiliation; and speak within strict time limits. Verbatim transcripts may be taken, often to become part of a legally supportable written document.

Informational meetings in community settings such as neighborhoods are less formal in structure than those before political decision makers in downtown civic buildings, but even they are characterized by a minimal amount of interaction among participants.

Though the environment and format of informational meetings are not receptive to surprises or creative ideas, some people find ways to break through.

> *In Oregon some time ago, State Senator Maurine Neuberger took a skillful detour from the common, dry style that characterizes most testimony and won an important political victory. Faced with the competing interests of a predominantly male state legislature whose members had little experience in the kitchen, a female constituency clamoring for a change in the law to allow grocers to sell colored margarine, and an influential dairy lobby that did not want margarine to compete with butter, Senator Neuberger orchestrated an effective show-and-tell.*
>
> *On the polished mahogany table of a crowded legislative hearing room, she placed paraphernalia that disgruntled housewives all over the state faced: mixing bowls and spoons, white margarine, and little packets of yellow food coloring. Donning an apron over her dress-for-success suit, she fussed with the concoction, finally coloring the margarine the only way it was then allowed in the state—mixed in a bowl with a heavy spoon. She then held up her messy results, having made her point effectively in front of her colleagues as well as the dozens of television, radio, and newspaper reporters she had alerted beforehand.*
>
> *Consumer groups readily joined the campaign, the dairy lobby dared not continue to oppose this onslaught of public opinion, and a law was passed to allow colored margarine to be sold in Oregon.*

The most common form of presentation at an informational meeting is one-way: one person at a time talks to a panel of listeners. This "talking head" approach need not be dry and monotonous, though it often is. Part of the problem is that many people who present the same type of information at several meetings make the mistake of following the one-format-fits-all approach. They fail to recognize that each audience and issue is different and requires a personalized presentation, or, at the least, a different introduction or orientation. This can be accomplished easily by reorganizing the material to emphasize the concerns of each particular audience.

> *In the matter of a new zoning ordinance that permits multiple-family dwellings in residential areas, a city board of supervisors is most interested in how the proposal affects the budget for the planning department, while residents in a middle-class neighborhood want to know primarily how it affects property values and traffic congestion. The downtown Rotary Club probably is more interested in how this may affect business. Wise presenters craft specific introductions that acknowledge the known concerns of each particular audience before presenting their other facts, which are the same for each meeting.*

As Figure 2.1 on page 15 shows, in the typical hearing format, the officials receiving the information are seated on a raised platform, well removed from the audience. Even if they are on the same level as the spectators, there is a noticeable distance between them.

If you are making a presentation to such a body, give it your primary attention, no matter how many people are passively watching the proceedings behind you. If possible, arrange the screen or charts at an angle so that they can be seen by both the public officials and the general public; but if you have to make a choice, the officials come first. One or more television monitors that convey the images to the audience are becoming more common and are well appreciated. Use handouts to emphasize particular points or to provide additional information that can be read later. Have a sufficient quantity for all the expected attendees.

If the dais is not fixed, a simple way to minimize the problem of presenters sitting or standing with their backs to the audience at an informational hearing is to move the decision makers from the center-front of the room to an angle off to one side (Figure 2.2 on page 17). Individual presenters then stand or sit sideways to them and the audience, giving the latter at least a partial view of everything that goes on.

No matter how diligently a conscientious presenter tries to mitigate the problem, the main drawback of an informational meeting is the we/they atmosphere it creates and perpetuates, as illustrated by the following incident.

The state parks commission staff set up the hearing room in a format—commission on a raised dais, staff and public below—they had used hundreds of times before. The purpose of the meeting was for staff people to provide information to the commission about options for new campgrounds. The ponderous and formal meeting process, with staff giving their set presentations, moved ahead for an hour or so, slowly fulfilling the stated purpose, until the commission chair noticed that an unusually large number of citizens had filled up every empty seat in the room.

After discreet inquiry of the staff, he was told that a contingent of people had traveled nearly 100 miles to be at the meeting, hoping that even though it was advertised as strictly informational, for the commission only, they would be allowed to testify about their community's concern for one of the park sites being considered. They had not tried to disrupt the proceedings until now, but they were obviously getting restless.

The chair called a short recess to consider the matter with his fellow commissioners, but without consulting staff. When the commissioners again took their seats on the dais, the chair acknowledged the audience by announcing that he was changing the purpose of the meeting. They had heard "enough canned information," he said in a benevolent manner that appealed to the audience but angered the staff. They would now open up the meeting for a half-hour of public comment.

The first citizen stood up. Ignoring the chair's request to identify herself, she launched into a tirade against the commission for showing slides of their community that the citizens could not see from their seats. A second person interrupted her, asking why the public was given only 30 minutes to presents its views while "staff has hours." When the meeting degenerated into a

Figure 2.1. Typical Informational Meeting or Hearing Format

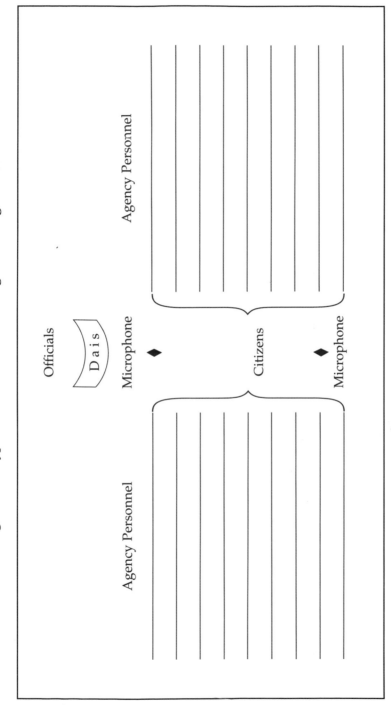

> *shouting match, the chair saw no other way out than to gavel it to adjournment. As the angry citizens shuffled out, some pausing at the door to argue with staff, and vow to take further action, the chair and his fellow commissioners shook their heads. "See what happens when we try to get a little citizen involvement? We'll never do that again."*

Unfortunately, they learned the wrong lesson from the experience. Seeking citizen involvement was not the culprit. Difficulties occurred when the chair abruptly tried to convert an informational meeting into an advisory or problem-solving meeting without changing the format and environment. The physical configuration was adequate for the planned staff informational presentation but inappropriate when the commission suddenly switched to soliciting public opinion. Some in the audience were seated behind posts and could not see the entire commission; others could not hear, because there were no microphones; and without an organized procedure for participation, anxious citizens resorted to shouting and waving their arms to be recognized. No wonder, then, that the meeting disintegrated. When the chair decided to change to an advisory mode, he should at the very least have adjourned the formal part of the session and moved the commission off the dais onto the same level as the audience. With more advance warning, staff people might have been able to reconvene the meeting in a room more suited to constructive dialogue.

In the panel discussion, a variation of the one-on-one approach to presenting information, there are several presenters rather than one, each with a discrete message to convey. They are usually seated on a raised platform facing an audience. The panel is an effective way to give equal attention to different aspects of a subject and invite controlled audience interaction. The decision makers or primary receivers may sit off to one side, in the front row, or among the public. To denote their special status, they may be given time to respond or ask questions before the general audience can participate. Verbatim notes are rarely taken, though speakers may provide written transcripts of their remarks.

The success of the panel discussion format in generating information depends on the skill of the moderator to move matters along and the ability of participants to communicate. (See Chapter 5 for details.)

Figure 2.2. Improved Informational Meeting or Hearing Format

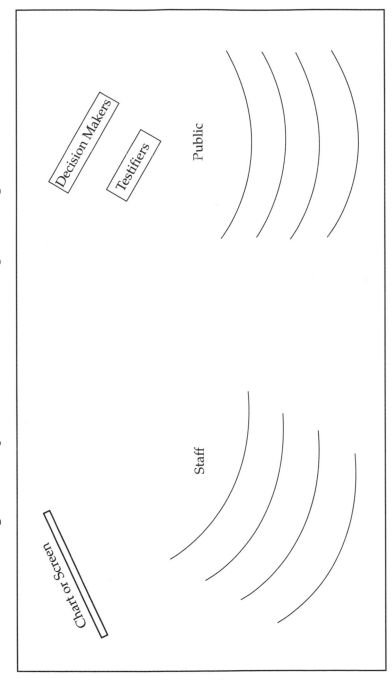

ADVISORY MEETINGS

As the middle ground between meetings that are primarily informational and those convened to solve problems, advisory meetings allow representatives of an agency or organization to present information in a public forum and invite non-binding advice on alternatives or a particular course of action. Thus, there is a structured two-way dialogue.

Advisory meetings fail when the public misunderstands their limitations and has unreasonable expectations of how citizens can influence the ultimate decision. The chair must present the ground rules clearly at the beginning, telling attendees how the results of this meeting will be used in the decision-making process. If there is a noticeable trickling in of latecomers, it is wise to repeat this so that they have no excuse for disrupting the meeting. ("No one told me we weren't going to be allowed to vote on this tonight.")

> *The state transportation director, warned by her alert staff that citizens might think that they were to make a decision about the controversial issue under discussion, wisely decided to be forthright as she called the public meeting to order. "As most of you know," she began, "the transportation commission has the legal responsibility to decide the location of the highway bypass, but we've called this meeting in advance of their meeting next month to hear from you. Where do you think the bypass should go, and why? We're keeping a written record of everything you say tonight, and that record will be available to the commission before they make a decision. It's been our experience that they consider citizen comments seriously, so what you say tonight is very important."*
>
> *The public played by the rules she laid out and proceeded, in orderly fashion, to make valuable comments that influenced the ultimate decision. It was obvious they were being heard, but it was also clear who the decision makers were.*

All advisory meetings should begin with a presentation of basic information, and either the talking head or panel discussion format is suitable. The workshop, a specific type of advisory meeting, discussed in the following problem-solving section, has public opinion components. Better still, however, is the community fair, a format that reaches out to and receives comments from a cross-section of the public in a two-way process of interaction and dialogue.

Sometimes called an open house, the community fair is designed to allow maximum participation by many citizens, provide ready access to technical information, and solicit oral and written comments that will be considered seriously by the sponsors before they make a decision. The format is uniquely suited to large-scale controversial projects, such as a comprehensive community plan or transportation alternatives, where a considerable amount of technical information must be conveyed to an audience with diverse interests and needs.

The community fair is oriented to the citizen rather than to the sponsor. It is a refreshing alternative to the typical public informational or advisory meeting, at which technicians and professionals go to considerable length to convey information and data, usually by giving overly long and detailed oral presentations to an increasingly restless audience.

As Figure 2.3 on page 21 illustrates, the community fair requires a large meeting room that can accommodate several activities simultaneously. School gymnasiums and cafeterias, senior and community centers, or church meeting halls are generally the most suitable.

As people enter the fair, they stop by the information desk to sign in and pick up an orientation packet, which includes a small map of the room layout, an agenda, and background material. It is important to urge everyone to sign in with name, address, phone number, fax, e-mail, so that the sponsors can have an accurate count. You may also offer to send them any follow-up material. Easy to-read signs mark the different areas of activity. Staff and/or officials of the sponsoring agency, identified with name tags, T-shirts, or caps, roam around the hall, greeting people and answering questions. As the purpose of the community fair is to meet citizens' needs, it must extend over several hours (from 4 to 8:30 p.m. works in most communities). The hosts may take turns at shifts of two to three hours each, but the person in charge is on duty the entire time.

The extended timespan is just one example of the citizen-friendly quality of the community fair. Seniors, students, retirees, or others who may be reluctant to go out at night can attend during the daytime, while working people can drop by in the early evening.

All fair activities take place simultaneously and continuously. Citizens are encouraged to stay as long as they like, moving at an individual pace between informational displays (to examine maps, charts, and handouts), resource tables (to ask questions of the technical experts), and perhaps a continuously running informational slide show or video.

To accommodate families, the community fair should have a children's corner staffed by a qualified caretaker, with coloring and story books and, if possible, some simple illustrative material on the subject under discussion. Child-friendly refreshments such as punch or juice and cookies, in addition to adult fare of tea and coffee, are served.

To enhance the goal of informed two-way interaction, the registration packet should include easy-to-read summaries of technical data and people should be encouraged to engage the "experts" in discussions of matters of particular concern. They also should be asked to write down their opinions at the various stations and fill out a questionnaire as they leave. Issues brought up during the individual discussions can be recorded on large sheets of butcher paper or newsprint tacked to walls or dividers near each resource table. If this open house is being combined with a formal hearing, a screened, separate section or room for oral testimony should be set aside. A court reporter also may be on hand to take verbatim testimony from citizens who do not have time to stay for a prolonged hearing.

The community fair format requires considerable staff commitment: Personnel must organize and send out notices; be present to set up, answer questions, provide information, and collect comments; and analyze the comments after the event. The time is well spent, however. The very openness of this format—sending the message that the agency or organization cares enough to meet the citizens on their own terms—creates a wellspring of positive community reaction. It also gives the sponsor the opportunity to obtain valuable advisory opinions on issues of importance.

> *Fifty thousand people, spread out over 200 miles in six counties in two states, were invited to participate, through several regional community fairs, in the planning process for a major river corridor that affected them all. To accommodate the diverse population of farmers and city dwellers, seniors and young families, the fairs*

Figure 2.3. Advisory Meetings in Community Fair Format

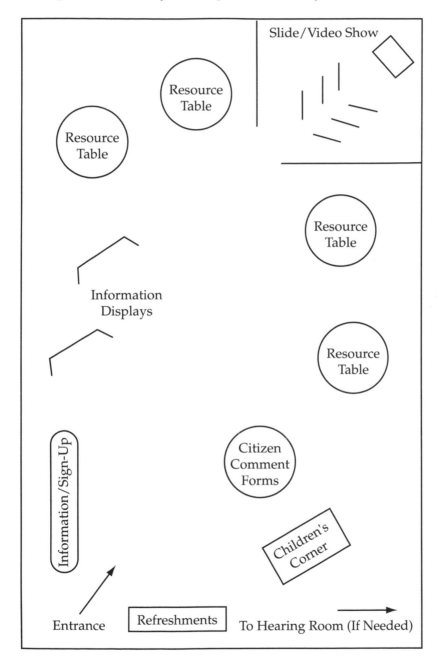

*were held in church meeting halls and school cafeterias
in each county from noon to 10 p.m. Citizens—many
with their families—came at their leisure, milled around,
met their neighbors, obtained information on issues of
particular concern, and voiced their opinions. Even
those adamantly opposed to any "government interven-
tion" grudgingly admitted that they had been treated
fairly and that they appreciated the agency's obvious
efforts to meet them more than halfway.*

PROBLEM-SOLVING MEETINGS

The purpose of a problem-solving meeting is to discuss a controversial or complex issue and reach agreement on a solution that all
or most participants can support. Those problem-solving public
meetings that encourage participants to find areas of common
agreement through consensus are less polarizing than those that
make decisions by vote where there are winners and losers. Voting
may be necessary, however, to provide closure on an issue where all
other methods have failed.

Every problem-solving meeting should begin with a summary of
the information that all participants need to know. Many managers
and directors make a common mistake that derails these meetings at
the outset: They assume that everyone knows the same basic information and agrees on what the issues are or they would not have
bothered to come to the meeting in the first place. Acting on this erroneous notion, organizers call the meeting to order and then launch
right into the discussion. To their dismay, they soon find that most citizen attendees possess little or even erroneous information, depend-
ing on their varying experiences and prejudices. People may rightly
balk at discussing the problems that the sponsor has identified until
they clear up ambiguities and misinformation or acquire what may
seem to be elementary facts. Heated arguments and debates ground-
ed on misunderstandings may prevent a problem-solving meeting
from ever getting to its purpose: open and fair discussion.

To avoid these dangers, the managers and staff people who plan
problem-solving meetings should structure the format so that the
first part of the agenda is a short show-and-tell, giving everyone the
same base of information. For a small group, a brief oral explanation
followed by a limited time for questions from the audience suffices.
Handouts that participants can read at their own pace also are help-

ful. For a large group—50 or more—the goal can be accomplished more effectively with the addition of a slide show, video, or simple graphics. All information should be as free from bias as possible and be expressed in clear, common, jargon-free terms.

If someone in the audience challenges the time spent on explanations ("Let's get on with the meeting. We've heard all this before!"), the chair may ask for a show of hands to indicate how many in the audience want to continue hearing the factual presentation. Usually the majority will vote to go on. If most people indicate they are sufficiently informed, skip the rest of the informational presentation and proceed to the discussion.

The problem-solving meeting is the most complicated of the three types, involving multiple levels of communication: leader to group, group to leader, group to group, and individuals to each other. Keeping it all going requires strong and alert leadership—a quick-witted and alert chair, who acts as the catalyst and convener, and one or more facilitators, who channel the energy and knowledge of the group in positive directions. In particularly complex situations, the facilitator should have mediation or negotiating skills.

A third important participant—optional in the other types of meetings but essential in all problem-solving sessions—is the recorder. (See Chapter 1.) The recorder is the keeper of the group memory, performing the neutral function of getting down the essence of what the group is saying.

The recorder's writing must be in full view of the participants at all times. In a large group, an overhead transparency may be more readable than even the darkest marking pen on butcher paper or newsprint.

Public agency staff people were surprised that more than 100 people turned out to help them reach consensus on one of three options for development standards for a proposed recreational area. Prepared for just a handful of citizens, the agency director had brought only a chart pack and marking pens.

Despite the large crowd that overwhelmed the room, he plunged ahead with his prepared remarks, summarizing his salient points by writing on a regular-sized chart with a colored pen that he had been assured was an "audience friendly" blue. Friendly it was, but so light that it was unreadable to anyone past the third row.

Some people sitting in the back of the room became quarrelsome and hostile. "Why are you writing so only the folks in front can see?" shouted one. "We're just as important as they are." Added another, "You're going to have to go over it again point by point. We want to know what you're writing."

In a smart move that averted total chaos and rebellion, the director apologized and called a short recess until a staff member could find a black marking pen. He did have to start over, but at least he knew that this time everyone in the group could follow along.

There would not have been even the potential for a citizen uprising if the organization had been more astute in its planning and prepared overheads in advance. Ready for a large group, they could have shifted over easily to a chart and pen if only a small group had come. (See Chapter 8, which covers audiovisuals.)

Given that its purpose is involving all participants in finding solutions to an issue or developing a supportable program or plan of action, the workshop is the best general format for discussions at a problem-solving public meeting. (Figure 2.4 on page 25) Though such meetings may appear formless to the latecomer or unpracticed eye, their success depends on being carefully organized and following a specific timetable and agenda. (As noted previously, a brief presentation of basic information should precede the public discussion phase.)

Though most problem-solving meetings are concerned with serious topics, organizers need not take a heavy approach. In fact, a light touch often works better.

The staff of a parks and recreation district in a growing suburban community was frustrated because one group of citizens harangued them for not being visionary enough to spend more on facilities while another wanted them to take a conservative, pay-as-you-go approach. Neither group wanted to exceed the budget; they just had different ideas about how to spend the money.

Finally, staff brought both factions together, challenging them to come up with a spending plan that the

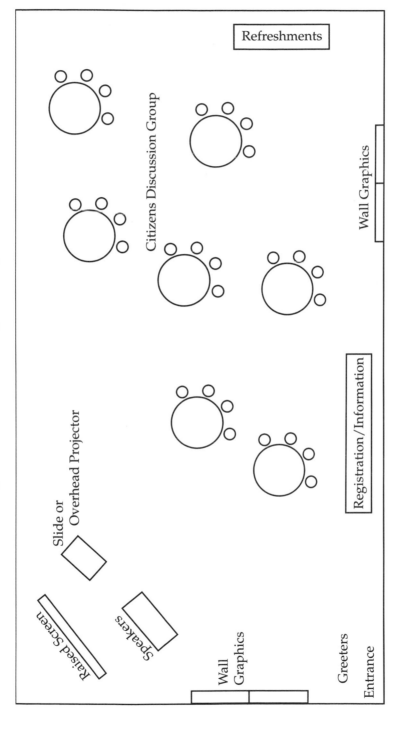

Figure 2.4. Problem-Solving Workshop Format

majority could accept. After a staff presentation about the current situation, the more than 100 vocal citizens were divided into groups of eight, with each group given $5 million in "play money"—the annual amount the district had to spend. Each group was then asked to agree on reasonable allocations not exceeding the total.

Using this "fun" gaming approach, participants experienced the same frustration that staff felt and had to negotiate seriously and agree on trade-offs, all the while enjoying themselves. The large group's final, reasoned consensus reflected this thoughtful process.

If there are more than 12 attendees, individuals should be assigned to smaller groups for the participatory interactive discussions that the workshop format requires. Eight to 12 people at each table is optimal for small-group discussions. With fewer than six it may not be easy to keep a discussion going; more than 12, and it is difficult to make sure that everyone is involved. The small groups may convene as a large body both before the discussion to hear the introductory information and afterwards to share their small-group findings and recommendations.

Everyone—speakers and audience—sits on the same physical level. Appropriate seating arrangements contribute to the dynamic, creative, synergistic environment that an ideal problem-solving workshop requires. Planners of the meeting should encourage people of disparate interests to sit together. With the proper facilitation, they learn from each other and begin to respect and accept differing points of view.

Meeting organizers must take an active hand to counter the natural tendency of people to sit with those they know or with whom they feel most comfortable. The easiest, most effective way to disperse the audience is by numbering each name tag to correspond with a discussion group and give the tags out in order as people sign in.

"John, according to the number on your name tag, you're at table four. Even though you're his wife, Mary, you can see that your tag says table five. Thanks for splitting up. We want to give you the chance to share your point of view with as many people as possible tonight."

Once the reason for this system is explained, most people accept it readily, even though they may not be overjoyed to be separated from their friends and relatives.

> *The public meeting was called to discuss school taxes, a contentious issue in that particular part of the state, and the antis and pros were out in force. Most people accepted their table assignments when they were handed numbered name tags, but one of the more aggressive spokespeople complained. "Our side needs to sit together to organize our strategy," he said.*
>
> *"I understand," said the chair, firmly but with a smile. "But we want to give everyone a chance to speak with people who might not agree with them. You may even convince some of the opposition of your point of view." The complainer reluctantly sat down where he was told. After a particularly lively and creative discussion, he admitted that the "enemy" did not look nearly as fierce face-to-face.*

An important result of small group discussions not to be overlooked is the quality and quantity of the information attendees provide. Only a relatively few people speak out in large group settings and they often are the most bold and opinionated. The small group discussion processes described here encourage people with wide differences of opinion to express themselves in non-threatening and accepting environments. Moreover, there is a greater opportunity for people with diverse opinions to learn from each other.

For advisory or decision-making purposes, it is more likely that a group consensus will emerge if people representing all the interests at the meeting are randomly dispersed at the various small discussion tables. Birds of a feather flocking together will agree with each to such a predictable degree that they can easily and quickly cause polarization and dissent that affects the reliability of the data and feedback generated. In other words, random seating will produce results that are more reflective of the group as a whole.

If at all possible, avoid using rectangular tables, especially in a large room that will have many discussions going on at once. People at one end may not be able to hear those at the other, nor can they maintain the personal eye contact and interaction important to good

Figure 2.5. Birds of a Feather Should Not Flock Together

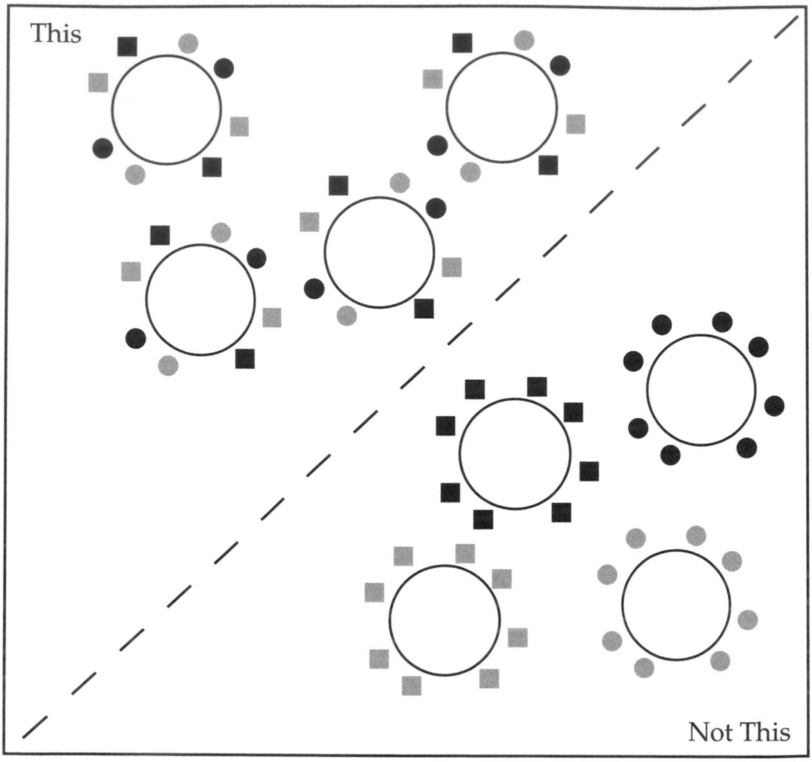

group dynamics. Round tables provide an environment more conducive to good discussion. School cafeterias are desirable locations for public meetings (see Chapter 5), in part because they usually have round tables. If you have to settle for the rectangular variety and acoustics are a problem, try to set up some groups in other rooms.

The discussion leader's seating choice also influences the dynamics of a problem-solving discussion. At a round table, wherever the leader sits becomes the "head." At a rectangular table, discussion leaders maintain the best control by sitting at one end so that they can be seen and heard easily by everyone. Some egalitarian facilitators shun the authoritative stance and sit in the middle of the long side of the table. This puts them at a disadvantage, however: They have to keep turning their heads to and fro to acknowledge various members of the group. The recorder should sit next to the discussion leader so that they can confer as matters arise.

In a problem-solving workshop, there are many ways to encourage meaningful, productive discussion and help people reach conclusions, consensus, or at the least, common ground. In all cases, the objective is to deliberate, not debate, have everyone participate in the discussion, and promote understanding of different perspectives. The appropriate method should be chosen in one of the first meeting-planning sessions, after you have agreed on the subject of the meeting and understand the knowledge and biases of the participants. Here are some of the more productive methods.

Brainstorming. An especially useful discussion technique, brainstorming protects shy members of a group from being bullied into submission by others more opinionated. It also gives a quick snapshot of everyone's central points of view.

The two ground rules of brainstorming are that everyone has a chance to say something and no idea is considered ridiculous or inappropriate. Going around the table, the discussion leader asks each party to say the first thing on this subject that comes to mind. (They may have been asked to jot down a few ideas before the discussion began.) Participants need not speak whole sentences; phrases or sentence fragments are acceptable, and sometimes even preferred. If there is considerable group energy, the leader may call for a second round of ideas, or even a third. The aim is to encourage all the new and creative thinking that the group is capable of without giving any loudmouth or bully an opportunity to take over.

After all the ideas—the more, the better—are recorded, on a paper and in handwriting large enough for all to see, participants are encouraged to embellish or build upon others' suggestions. In further steps in the brainstorming process, the group winnows down the list, combines, discards, and finally agrees on a manageable set of goals, objectives, or action statements as required by the meeting agenda. Discussion of trade-offs and consequences may be part of this or later discussions.

Visioning. This technique is often used as an icebreaker, though many organizations or communities engage in visioning as an independent process over many months. For purposes of this discussion, it involves asking participants to respond to a futuristic question such as, "Imagine us five (10, 15, etc.) years into the future. Describe what (our community, school, organization, etc.) should be like. Do not be concerned with financial or other constraints. Be imaginative. Describe your ideal world." Unless visioning is the purpose of the overall process, the discussion can then move on to the realities of how we can reach this ideal.

Reacting. Sometimes called the nominal group technique, reacting works well when the sponsors of the meeting first promulgate a set of principles or options that they ask a group to discuss. It is also a good technique by which to focus a heterogeneous group on a common objective, and requires a group of manageable size, no more than 25. Participants are given pens and paper and asked to write down their highest priority values, options, programs, or projects from among all those proposed by the sponsors. The facilitator then goes around the group and asks for everyone's first suggestion, second, and so on. This technique encourages people to do their own private thinking before participating and structures the discussion, making it less likely to stray. As a more formalized approach than brainstorming, it may lead to more specific conclusions. It also requires all members to participate—at least to the extent of reading from their lists—and may give them the incentive to defend their opinions later on.

Buzz groups. In buzz groups, as in brainstorming, participants are asked to bring to the table as many ideas as they can think of, but in buzz groups, they are encouraged to ask questions or suggest issues that require clarification or further discussion from "experts." This technique works well when a relatively uninformed group needs to understand complicated issues before meaningful discussion can take place. The leader may say, "Let's record all your questions and the issues that you don't understand. Then we'll ask the resource people to explain." It also requires a sufficient number of informed experts who can explain technical issues in terms laypeople can understand.

SWOT analyses. After a group has defined the issues and possible solutions, there may be a need to agree on a priority list. One way to focus the group's attention from many to few is to discuss the solutions in terms of their strengths, weaknesses, opportunities and barriers or threats, hence the acronym, SWOT. The operative question after these are identified is, "How do we make the most of our strengths and opportunities and overcome our weaknesses or barriers?" This exercise helps bring the discussion to closure.

Issue stations. When several items need to be addressed in some depth, each can be assigned to a separate table, under the general umbrella of the subject at hand. A specialist for each issue serves as the technical or topical resource, aided by a facilitator and recorder. Participants move freely among the tables, staying no longer than a predetermined time, when a bell or other signal indicates it is time to move on to another issue; recorders keep a record of the ongoing discussions. After an hour or two of these intense discussions, when participants have covered several issue tables, everyone convenes in a large group. The facilitators summarize what has been said at their tables; there is further discussion and possibly group consensus. This differs from the open house or community fair discussed previously because attendees are expected to be present and participate the entire time.

Rotating experts. As a substitute for a single informational presentation to one large audience, resource people can rotate among small groups, presenting their information to each one in turn. The more intimate environment encourages people who might be intimidated by a large format to express their opinions and question the experts. Following each presentation, the small groups, guided by their facilitators, discuss the issues and try to reach consensus.

Charrette. This can be effective when a community or neighborhood is concerned with an issue that affects many people and has many components, such as how to reconfigure or lay out a geographical area to meet public needs. The project could be a bike or pedestrian path, open space, public building, shopping area, or homes. A charrette requires professionals skilled in working with people and a considerable commitment of time by all the participants. It usually takes place over several days, or perhaps a weekend, and may involve several hundred citizens. The product usually is very graphic, such as a design for a new town plaza, but it may also be a written narrative about a specific set of principles or guidelines.

> *The downtown area of a small college town was deteriorating while the community around it was growing, with new homes and schools. In fact, even the college had a record enrollment. After several unsuccessful tries at asking the voters for more funds to fix up the ailing core area, the city hired an urban design and planning firm, which suggested a week-long design charrette.*
>
> *Over five days, from 6 to 9 p.m. each weekday evening, the community was invited to meet with the consultants at the senior center to work together on*

schemes to improve downtown. Citizen participants were asked to commit to coming the entire week, but in reality, most attended about three of the five sessions. Attendance increased as the week went on and word got around that citizens' ideas were actually being taken into account.

Using many of the techniques discussed in this chapter, including brainstorming and visioning, the consultants gave form to the many ideas by drawing them on large sheets of paper on which a map of downtown, with existing buildings, streets, and landmarks, had been printed. Middle and high school students came with their teachers during a school day to give their ideas. A political science class at the college also participated.

By week's end, a consensus on a revitalizing scheme for downtown emerged. A 21-member citizen steering committee was appointed by the city council to take further steps.

Whatever techniques are used, either singly or in combination, the facilitator must eventually ask the group to make choices or come to a conclusion. This step should be a natural outcome of the process of discussion. In one positive approach that does not polarize discussants, the facilitator summarizes on newsprint or large chart paper all the choices that the group has suggested and asks participants to talk about the advantages and disadvantages of each. This is less structured than the SWOT analysis discussed earlier while keeping the participants focused on consequences and tradeoffs. If the discussion is framed in these terms rather than in absolutes of yes or no, even the most stubborn members of the group may see other points of view, making accommodation and consensus more likely: "We can all have something to say about advantages, even if we don't support a particular item," the facilitator can explain.

Another way to help the group make choices is to introduce some fun into the process. List all the options or alternatives on a large chart and give everyone a few colored stick-on dots with which to "vote" for their choices. People take this exercise very seriously while appreciating the anonymity that the dots give them. The dots tell the story quickly and clearly; the choices of the group are instantly recognizable.

If you want to gather additional opinions and test for concepts and ideas that people may have been reluctant to express verbally, ask all participants to complete a short questionnaire before they leave the meeting.

The questionnaire should ask participants to rate the extent to which the meeting met their expectations as well as give them a further opportunity to express their opinions about the issues under discussion. Encourage participants to fill them out before they leave because very few will make the effort to mail them afterwards. Have them collated and analyzed before your post-meeting evaluation (Chapter 9). The information gleaned from these questionnaires is another important insight into the concerns and opinions of those at the meeting. While we recognize that this is not a statistically accurate reflection of public opinion, it is a valuable supplement to the wealth of feedback collected during the discussion.

The type of meeting and discussion processes you choose should advance the purpose of holding successful public meetings: help people understand choices and consequences, examine all points of view, and reach mutually supportable conclusions.

3

Getting the Word Out

Citizen-unfriendly notices are common roadblocks to successful public meetings. If you have experienced sparse attendance at your last few meetings, do not hide behind the excuse, "Well, we did what we could to get people to come; they just don't care." They will care and they will come if you contact those most affected and they understand the purpose of the meeting, what the outcome means to them, how their attendance can make a difference, and the role they are expected to play in the decision-making process.

Public agency managers should not justify poorly written or unclear notices on the grounds of statutory requirements: "The lawyers make us do it." While they cannot ignore the necessary legalese, they can direct their staff members to use understandable, concise English, and even to provide a translation into another language if the audience warrants it. Meeting planners who do not have any regulatory restrictions can be more creative in their notices.

> *The administrator of a midsize city was anxious to include its growing Hispanic population in a communitywide visioning process, but previous efforts to involve people whose first language was not English had failed. A local parish priest suggested that they print flyers and other material in Spanish and he would see that they were well distributed. The first translation failed because it was written by a college Spanish professor and was not in the vernacular used by most of these descendants of people from Mexico. A second version by a bilingual*

> *community leader was more accepted.*
>
> *City leaders were pleased to find that many more Hispanic people participated in the process, and even more importantly, this carried over into many positive reactions and appreciation for the special efforts that had been made to reach out to them.*

Before composing any meeting notice that will be delivered to the public, give thought to what people need to know to be motivated to attend. This factor must take precedence over what you think they should know or what you are required by law to tell them. The information should be presented in the general order given below.

- *Purpose of the meeting.* Citizens rightly become distressed if they show up at a meeting expecting an open session at which they can give testimony only to be told that just the staff and "expert witnesses" are allowed to speak. Similarly, the public will feel cheated if the notice leads people to believe that a definitive decision will be made before the meeting ends and they find that the purpose of the meeting is to gather opinions for a later decision to be made behind closed doors. Managers must make sure that everyone participating in the meeting understands its purpose; the first step is stating that purpose accurately in the written notice. Experiment with attention-getting headlines: "Street-Widening Proposal" will encourage more citizens to read on than the bureaucratic "Notice for Potential Vacation of Certain Streets for Purposes of Accommodating Traffic."

> *A council of governments in a growing metropolitan area was having trouble getting elected officials to attend a series of meetings titled "Urban Issues that Confront Us." When they sent out a notice announcing a "Summit Meeting to Solve Our Pressing Regional Problems," the attendance doubled.*

- *Action to be taken.* What will happen as the result of this meeting? More meetings? Definite recommendations? A tax increase? Be clear and unambiguous.
- *Date, time, and place.* Do not bury this information somewhere

toward the end of the notice; put it right up front. Recipients can thus consult their calendars and be spared having to read further if they are busy at the appointed time. On the other hand, with the purpose of the meeting stated so clearly and compellingly in the first paragraph, followed by the date, time, and place, they may decide to change their schedules because of the importance of the event.

- *Financial implications.* What, if anything, will the proposal under consideration cost? Will this street widening, annexation, park acquisition, solid-waste regulation, or other matter require the public to pay more money? Say so, and in terms that taxpayers can understand. Translate property tax millage rates and other esoteric jargon into potential taxes for a typical middle-class household or, if you are talking about sales or excise taxes, into so much per dollar of purchase.

- *Citizen participation.* Are ad hoc comments acceptable, or must people sign up in advance to testify? Can they register by mail to speak? Is there a time limit? Failure to make all the rules clear in the notice may cause misunderstanding and hostility that will ruin the public meeting. If citizens accidentally or purposely misunderstand their role and insist, "No one told us that we have only three minutes apiece," the agency director can point out the clear, unambiguous statement to that effect in the invitation.

- *Optional additional explanatory material.* Attach simple maps or charts to help people visualize complicated matters. If there are several illustrations, employ consistent symbols such as crosshatching and shading. Always include a north arrow and clearly mark streets or other familiar landmarks. In land-use matters, do not pass on a surveyor's dim pencil sketch annotated with scrawled notations that are impossible for laypeople to decipher.

- *Legal reference.* Include legal justification only if you must—preferably as an attachment that citizens can ignore if they wish without missing anything important.

Put all the above (with the exception of legal requirements, maps, and other extras) on one double-spaced page. If you hold many meetings using the same general outline, the notice can be standardized on the computer so that staff can just fill in the blanks. Remember to avoid verbosity, acronyms, and jargon. Give careful attention to format: wide margins, short paragraphs, and double-spaced text increase the likelihood that your notice will be read and taken seriously.

Keep lists current. It does little good to have a readable notice if your mailing list is inadequate or out-of-date. It is indefensible if you fail to notify all citizens you are legally required to contact because of faulty record keeping, even if the blame lies with the assessor's or auditor's office. But it is almost equally important to communicate with those who are likely to be interested but whom you are not legally required to notify, such as neighbors who live farther away than the statutory distance, citizens who have shown a previous concern for the issue, community leaders, and special-interest organizations. If the matter is controversial, resist the temptation to notify only those required to by law or known supporters of the issue. Ignoring opponents by not inviting them is foolhardy. They can use it against you in another forum. "Why didn't you tell us in time?" is an all too familiar, alas, all too true, mantra.

You may need to keep several mailing lists, divided according to subject, known concerns or interests, geographical location, and other important factors. But people move and organizational leaders change. Be sure to update your lists at least annually. An effective way to keep track of peripatetic constituents is to mail your notices first-class, with a notation that you will pay the postage for any undelivered mail returned to your office. That service is more expensive than one-way, third-class mail, of course, but it pays dividends in giving you confidence you have done as much as possible through the mails.

Another way to reach people is to ask civic or service organizations to insert your notice in their mailings, or at least to apprise their members of the upcoming event.

To reach a wide, somewhat undefined public not accessible through mailed notices, consider producing colorful flyers or posters—legal notices nailed to utility poles do not count!—that can be displayed at community and senior centers, shopping malls, and other places people congregate. If your organization has a web site or an e-mail list, post the meeting notice there. Take advantage of any local access or community cable television bulletin boards. In other words, use all available means to contact your likely audience.

Figure 3.1   Hearing Notification with a Light Touch.

WE'RE COMING DOWN THE MOUNTAIN
FOR A
PUBLIC BRIEFING
ON THE NATIONAL FOREST
ENVIRONMENTAL IMPACT STATEMENT
FOR A PROPOSED NEW SKI RESORT

*YOU AND OTHER MEMBERS OF YOUR
ORGANIZATION ARE INVITED TO ATTEND A
PRESENTATION WITH REPRESENTATIVES OF ALL THOSE
STUDYING THE PROPOSED
DEVELOPMENT PLAN. THEY WILL EXPLAIN
THE OPTIONS, THE PROCESS OF PREPARING
THE ENVIRONMENTAL IMPACT STATEMENT,
AND THE ROLE OF PUBLIC COMMENT.*

PLEASE JOIN US AT EITHER OR ALL OF THESE BRIEFINGS:

NOVEMBER 16   CHARLIE'S RESTAURANT, WINTERVALE

NOVEMBER 20   NATIONAL FOREST OFFICE

DECEMBER 6   ROOM A, CIVIC CENTER

ALL MEETINGS ARE BETWEEN 7:30 AND 9:30 P.M.
THEY ARE JOINTLY SPONSORED BY THE U.S. FOREST
SERVICE AND THE SKI RESORT.

> *The city council was anxious that all the small community's citizens be apprised of an important open house to consider proposed changes to the proposed comprehensive land-use plan. On advice of a citizen member of the planning commission, the council invested $150 in a 15-foot banner, hanging it on the outside of city hall, facing the most well-traveled street. Everyone who passed through saw the sign, and many commented on it favorably as the reason they came to the open house.*

Redundancy is an asset when you want to notify the public of an important meeting. The various methods discussed in this chapter are not mutually exclusive and many can be used in tandem to achieve maximum effectiveness. Whichever you choose, try to keep your message light. As Figure 3.1 on page 39 illustrates, taking a less serious tone can be an effective way of engaging the attention of the public without diminishing the seriousness of the subject.

The words, "We're coming down the mountain" set the right tone for this meeting on a controversial development issue; they indicate that, unlike most bureaucrats, these agency people are willing to meet with people on their own turf. Note that one of the meeting locations is Charlie's Restaurant. The U.S. Forest Service balked when this nontraditional site was first proposed but accepted it when friendly citizens insisted that it was the only common gathering place in this small mountain community. By the way, this was the most successful of the three public meetings.

The following two exhibits illustrate all the points discussed in this chapter. Figure 3.2 on page 41 is a notification form currently in use by a planning and zoning agency somewhere in the United States. A clearer, simpler, more citizen-friendly version of the same notice appears in Figure 3.3 on page 41.

If the first notice seems perfectly fine to you, step into the citizens' shoes for a moment. It fits all the legal requirements, to be sure, but it contains ambiguities, redundancies, and legalisms certain to confuse and perhaps antagonize the average person. The revision, keeping all the salient points but written in lay language, is more likely to be understood.

In addition to being helpful to the public and setting the scene for productive and effective public meetings, clear and concise notifications have another value: they reduce the number of annoying

Figure 3.2 Traditional Notification Form.

Notice of Hearing to Rezone Property

Regarding Petition No. 1789222 PB, related to former Petition No. 5589167 PB, tax parcel 089507-214-576. The city is entertaining said petition from Thomas McIntire, owner of property at 2900 Elm Street, to rezone said property from RS-2, Single-Family Residential, to PS-1, Public Service.

The first public hearing on this petition will be held by the city's Planning and Zoning Commission on February 28 at 6:30 P.M. in the third-floor auditorium of city hall. The second public hearing will be held by the planning and zoning commission on March 9 at 6:30 P.M. in the third-floor auditorium of city hall.

Following these public hearings, the Planning and Zoning Commission will either vote to instruct the City Attorney to draft a new zoning ordinance for this property, deny the petition, or continue the hearing in order to obtain additional comments and information.

The permitted uses for this property are single-family dwellings and customary accessory buildings incidental thereto. The permitted uses of the proposed zoning are libraries, senior and community centers, museums and art galleries, and public golf courses. Petitioner proposes to erect a senior or community center.

As a property owner within 400 feet of said property, you may make your views known to the Planning and Zoning Commission by appearing in person at one or both of said hearings or writing a letter to be received on or before the date of the second hearing. Other citizens may also testify.

If you have any questions or desire to review this request in detail, contact the Department of Planning and Zoning, City Hall, Room 725, or call 811-555-1155.

Figure 3.3. Revised Notification Form.

Proposal to Change Use of Residential Property to Allow Senior or Community Center *[Attention-getting title]*

Thomas McIntire, living at 2900 Elm Street, is asking the city to rezone his property from residential use (RS-2) to PS-1, to allow construction of a senior or community center. *[Purpose of the meeting]*

The city's planning and zoning commission may either allow or deny this request and is holding two public hearings to obtain citizen comments. *[Action to be taken]*

Both hearings will be held in the third-floor city hall auditorium, February 28 and March 9, at 6:30 P.M. *[Date, time, and place early in the notice]*

If the property is approved as proposed, it will be used by a nonprofit corporation, which will not pay property taxes. The remaining property taxpayers in the city will be required to make up the difference. The current property taxes paid by the owner are approximately $1,500 per year. *[Financial implications]*

All citizens who own property within 400 feet of this property are invited to testify in person or write to the department of planning and zoning before midnight of the second hearing, March 9. Any other interested parties may also participate in the hearing or in writing. *[Citizen participation]*

For more information, contact Hortense Allen, project planner, Department of Planning and Zoning, City Hall, Room 725, or call Ms. Allen at 811-555-5656. *[Optional additional information]*

Please refer to accompanying map for specific site information. The legal petition for this case is on file as #1789222 PB and #5589167 PB. *[Legal reference]* phone calls from citizens who are not proficient in bureaucratic gob-bledygook.

The first hint that citizens have of a public meeting is usually a written notice. Thus, it is counterproductive to use legal require-ments as an excuse for being obscure or misleading. Communicate with the right people clearly and concisely, using other languages in addition to English if needed, and you will be well rewarded. Planners of public meetings who do not have to consider legal notice restrictions can be even more imaginative.

If you have the budget, paid advertising can pay off in getting your meeting notice to more people. But do not skimp on profes-sional help in writing and graphics. This is sometimes included in the price of newspaper ads. Public agencies or organizations spon-soring public events often can convince local radio and television stations to provide free or reduced cost public service announce-ments, or PSAs.

Getting the word out is an important step in the whole rubric of holding successful meetings, but like everything else, it should be planned and carried out with care.

4

Creating the Right Environment for Each Meeting

It is 7:20 on a warm summer evening, 10 minutes before the public meeting to discuss a proposal to widen a nearby freeway is scheduled to begin. Already, a dozen citizens are milling around outside the local high school. Inside, behind the locked doors, frantic staff people hurriedly bustle about, trying to set up things in a gymnasium none of them has seen before.

The agency manager realizes that she forgot to assign anyone to be in charge of registration, so she asks her already overworked assistant to set things up, directing him to a shoe box jammed with name tags, pencils, marking pens, and miscellany from their last public meeting. Two other staff people push together chairs and tables that were scattered throughout the room, another adjusts the slide projector and screen, while someone else searches for an electrical outlet for the coffee maker. The display charts fall down just as quickly as they are put up. To their chagrin, staff members realize that masking tape does not hold on concrete gym walls—but they do not have anything else.

Someone discovers that the projector bulb has burned out and hurriedly leaves by a side door to drive over to a nearby shopping mall, hoping to find a photography or hardware store still open.

The manager wipes her sweaty brow and looks up at the clock. "Okay, team, it's 7:29. Ready or not, one more minute and we'd better let them in."

The crowd outside has grown. "This is a public building. They can't lock us out," one citizen is heard to grumble. When the assistant opens the door, people rush in, many hurrying by the registration table without picking up their name tags or explanatory material. A line has formed by the coffee pot, which is just beginning to perk, while several others complain that it's just like "them" to serve a scalding drink when they should have had cold punch in the middle of summer.

At 7:45, everything is more or less ready—except that the slide projector now lacks both a bulb and an operator. The manager decides to begin anyway. "We're 15 minutes late already," she says. "I'll just tell everyone that we've cut out the slides because we're starting so late. Okay, let's wing it."

And "wing it" they do—through the entire awful evening. It is not until 10:30 that the last frustrated citizen straggles out and the exhausted public officials pack up to go home.

This meeting was programmed for disaster from the moment the agency manager and staff arrived—too late to cope with unfamiliar facilities and too rushed to handle inevitable last-minute problems such as the burned-out bulb. A seasoned manager might have been able to make a mid-course correction and hold a moderately successful session, but it would have been difficult given the environmental obstacles she and her staff were ill-prepared to handle, even though they had chosen an acceptable location.

An important but often neglected key to the success of any public meeting is a positive, welcoming environment that sets the stage for the program that follows. The following specific factors require attention.

SATISFACTORY SITE

Realtors are fond of saying that the three major factors that influence the marketability of a piece of property are location, location, and location. The same can be said of a successful public meeting. When planning your meeting, choose a site convenient and acceptable to the majority of attendees. What place is most well known and easily reached by the public you are inviting? Accessible to people with special needs such as the elderly and handicapped? With adequate parking? Close to transit? Safe and well lighted?

Schools often meet these criteria. Most people are familiar with the location of their neighborhood schools and have a generally favorable, or at least neutral, feeling about them. Make sure, however, that there is ample seating for adults. Sitting for a half-hour or more in a primary school chair will upset even the most sanguine citizen.

Senior or community centers and church and synagogue meeting rooms—not religious sanctuaries, lest we are accused of mixing the secular with sacred—also are good places for public meetings. They are usually in well-known, accessible locations and tend to have ample parking. A word of caution: Acquaint yourself with the religious institutions in each neighborhood or community to be sensitive to any rivalries or interdenominational quarrels that may make some attendees uncomfortable and cause other people to stay away.

Senior and community centers, schools, and churches have other advantages as well. They usually have large, flexible rooms, ample tables and chairs, screens and microphones, and friendly and accommodating custodians—the latter are a real plus when and if anything goes wrong. Another plus: The charges for using such facilities are minimal. But do not let finances alone dictate your choice. Your local courthouse or city hall may be a cost-free site, for example, but neither would be an ideal location for a public meeting if the people affected live miles away and are averse to coming downtown.

Government facilities, such as hearing rooms or council chambers, present other problems. With their typical raised dais and fixed audience seating, they have a physical inflexibility and formality that discourage dynamic group interaction. This environment, which purposely encourages proper decorum and order at governmental meetings, is not conducive to the creativity and frankness necessary when citizens are called together to discuss, debate, or come to consensus on public issues.

It is best to avoid private meeting rooms in banks or large businesses as well—these may be too upscale and intimidating for ordinary citizens. Hotels are the least favorable locations for effective public meetings, though they may have good parking. They either cost too much or give the aura of costing too much. When a nearby school or church is free (or nearly so), a public agency cannot risk being accused of wasting taxpayers' money by paying for a hotel conference room—even if the most expensive hotel in town is giving you a special price. In addition, hoteliers are in the hospitality, not the meeting, business. If they provide the room free, they will charge mightily for refreshments, microphones, screens, or any extras. Moreover, the partitions that separate large meeting areas into smaller units are usually flimsy and far from soundproof, and you cannot control who might be holding a meeting next door.

> *After a long search, the agency executive and staff chose a downtown hotel for their public meeting on proposed new environmental standards because it was in a central location and citizens were expected to come from a large geographical area. Just as the meeting started, they were dismayed to hear band music coming out of the loudspeaker. The executive complained to the hotel manager, who just shrugged his shoulders. "Sorry," he said, "but that's not piped-in music. The steamfitters' union is having its annual dinner dance next door to you. Since you didn't reserve that room, we gave it to them. The band will take a break in an hour," he added.*

One of the reasons the hotel had been chosen in the first place was because the manager was on the planning commission and had offered the room "free." The agency was dismayed later to receive a hefty bill of $32 for each flip chart and stand and $100 for each of several microphones.

VISIBLE SIGNS

Even if you have chosen a well-known, accessible location, never assume that people will know where to go once they get there.

Always post large and visible directional signs in the parking area, on the outside of the building, by the entry door, and on the inside, pointing to the specific meeting room. Take extra cardboard arrows with you to provide proper direction.

> *A state legislative committee holding a series of local hearings in a widespread geographical area chose nearby*

community colleges, because, as the chair insisted, "Everyone knows where they are." He was half-right. Everyone knew where the colleges were, but once there, especially at night, people were quickly lost. All the buildings looked alike. Directional signs helpful to knowing students were confusing to unfamiliar citizens, and most parking areas were off-limits to visitors.

Luckily, the manager who organized these meetings made sure that these problems were solved ahead of time. Inspecting each site several weeks before, staff members noticed how visitor-unfriendly they were. Back at the office, they hand-lettered directional signs and arrows and mounted them at all the entry points, marking a clear route to the meeting room. The invitations and advertisements included a small map of the campus and indicated where guest parking was allowed. Each meeting got off to a good start when several participants thanked staff members for making it so easy to get there.

CONVENIENT TIMING

You must also avoid the common error of scheduling a public meeting for the convenience of the sponsors rather than the audience. It may be customary to conduct official business on weekdays from 8 a.m. to 5 p.m., but those hours are not convenient for any but the retired or the most committed citizen. Choose the time for your public meeting when most of the public can attend—7 or 7:30 on a weekday evening is best, although a weekend morning or late afternoon sometimes works. Know the mores and customs of your community or audience and plan accordingly.

Innovative community leaders in a predominantly Catholic neighborhood hold successful community forums from 9 a.m. to 4 p.m. on Saturdays, with breaks for Mass or just relaxation. They find that citizens in this area are less tired and distracted at that time than during the work week and are willing to give up part of their weekends to discuss important civic issues.

However, a meeting called on a Saturday in a primarily Jewish or Seventh-Day Adventist community would bomb, because Saturday is the Sabbath for these groups.

Likewise, in some communities Wednesday night is church night. Though not everyone is at Bible study or choir rehearsal, those who are not stay close to home.

WELCOME REFRESHMENTS

Food is a hospitable touch that has put many a potentially contentious meeting on a civilized track. A pleasant conviviality ensues when people have the opportunity to chat over a cup of hot coffee or tea or, on a particularly warm evening, a glass of cold punch. If the facility itself cannot make refreshments available, check out a local caterer or reasonably priced delivery beverage service. Though not mandatory, cookies are a nice addition. They often can be obtained as a donation from a nearby bakery or supermarket if you give the donor recognition on the program or post a small, tasteful notice on the table.

The citizens who came to discuss Department of Ecology plans to change the course of a nearby stream gathered beforehand in small, friendly groups around the refreshment table. Then, someone noticed that foam cups were being used for the beverages. The subject of banning such non-biodegradable items in public places was a hot community topic just then, and many of these environmentally aware people were outraged. They not only boycotted the liquid refreshments, but loudly denounced their hosts for not being more sensitive.

The department supervisor vainly pleaded innocence; "someone" had unthinkingly ordered the service from the catering company. Failure to consider an important community value canceled out any of the pluses that the agency might have derived from providing the refreshments.

ROOM WITH NO VIEWS

You have chosen the proper external environment. The location, date, and time are acceptable to most, and there is ample parking and nearby public transit. You have set a convivial atmosphere with simple refreshments. All to the good.

The next concern is the room itself. It must be suitable in size and arrangement to further the goals of the meeting. First decide what you want to accomplish and then choose the setting that helps you meet your aims. What is the purpose of the meeting? To impart information only? To receive information only? Impart and receive? Discuss issues? Solve problems? Reach consensus or a decision? Build goodwill? The wrong setup may create an environment that makes it impossible, or at the least very difficult, to attain your objectives.

The sloped floors and fixed seats of a college lecture hall work well when there is one expert (the professor) and less learned and captive receivers (students). It is a deadly configuration for any meeting at which public interaction is desired. If you are holding such a meeting at a college, choose a room with movable seats and where everyone is on the same level.

All meeting rooms should have the following features:

- Size adequate for the number of people expected—but able to be enlarged or divided if more or fewer attend.
- Few or no distractions, such as scenic views or reflecting windows.
- As little distance as possible between presenters and audience.
- Good acoustics and sight lines so that all attendees can hear and see without straining.
- Comfortable chairs and tables, but not so cushy that people can fall asleep with impunity. (They may fall asleep anyway, but you do not want to make it easy for them!)
- Adequate and usable wall space for posters, charts, maps, and other explanatory material.
- Ample, clean nearby restrooms.
- Environment that encourages a creative and cordial exchange of views.

> *City planners had come several miles out to a newly annexed area to talk with the citizens about a controversial sewer construction project. Expecting much public interest, they had scheduled six meetings in different high and middle school gymnasiums: big barn-like rooms that could easily hold several hundred people. To their dismay and chagrin, the four citizens who came to the first meeting were easily outnumbered by the six city personnel. The supervisor wisely decided to alter the*

auditorium-style arrangement and invited people up to the front of the room where they had hurriedly set up two folding tables.

In this impromptu setting, planners and citizens sat around one table, engaging in an animated conversation. The staff members abbreviated their planned remarks and invited questions as they went along. When the seating configuration was changed and bureaucrats and citizens could see eye to eye, the environment also changed—from suspicious and wary to open and cordial. In fact, this meeting was more successful than the others with higher attendance. Many creative ideas to help people deal with the dreaded inconvenience the sewer project was sure to bring were suggested and eventually adopted.

Size flexibility works both ways, of course. What if you plan a meeting for 25 people and 250 show up? Be prepared! Whenever, possible, make sure that everyone has a seat, even if you have to drag in chairs from other parts of the building—still another good reason to use a church or a school. They usually have plenty of extra folding chairs and various-sized meeting rooms. Citizens will be good natured about a little crowding as long as they can see and hear.

Consider using school or public libraries or media centers when the subject of the meeting is likely to draw strong-minded advocates. Carpeted floors and book-lined walls tone down the rhetoric of even the most dedicated rabble-rousers.

The staff committee assigned to setting up the room for the first economic development advisory committee arrived at a neighborhood school early and began to unload charts and graphs. The accommodating school maintenance man had been contacted earlier and was there to unlock the front door and show them to the room they had reserved, next to the gymnasium.

"Here it is, I set up the tables just like you asked for. I hope that the music won't bother you too much," he said. "What music?" asked the startled coordinator. "Why, the 200-voice church choir that rehearses in the gym every Wednesday night," he answered. The startled coordinator exclaimed, "We can't meet next door to that.

No one told us about them." "Well, I guess no one asked," answered the maintenance man.

The coordinator thought quickly. There was no way to change the meeting time or place, people would begin arriving in about 90 minutes. But the school had many other available rooms, and with the maintenance man's help, they were able to move the meeting to the media center on the other side of the building. They hurriedly rearranged this new room and posted directional signs all over the building. The exuberant choir could still be heard, but the sound was muffled. The chair laughingly referred to the unexpected serenade as the reason for changing the location and it was an ice breaker that helped relieve tension at the beginning of the meeting.

NECESSARY NAME TAGS

Name tags are an easy if unimaginative way to create a friendly environment. Never assume everyone knows everyone else, and they are handy memory joggers in any case. But test them out before the meeting and use only those that can be removed easily. Some sticky-backed tags can pull off bits of fabric and may justifiably anger users. Banks and utilities often provide name tags free— printed with their logos, of course. If you want staff and elected officials to be easily recognizable, give them different-colored name tags. On the other hand, if you or they prefer not to stand out from the general public, have them wear the same color as everyone else.

Make sure that all attendees receive name tags as they sign in. If you see people slip into the room without them, seek them out and ask them to wear one unless they are visibly uncomfortable identifying themselves. In meetings where it is important to distribute people randomly, name tags can serve another purpose: They can be pre-numbered so that attendees are automatically assigned to sit at a numbered table that matches their name tag.

FAIL-SAFE EQUIPMENT

Provide pencils and pads at any meeting at which citizens are likely to want to write anything down, and take care that your audiovisual equipment does what it is expected to do. As we saw at the beginning of this chapter, a seemingly inconsequential matter such as the lack of a spare projector bulb can upset an entire agenda.

Well before the audience arrives, test all your equipment—slides, overheads, videos, microphones—in the room in which you will be holding the meeting. If the public address system has feedback or other problems, find the maintenance person or ask someone on your staff to help. A dress rehearsal of your slides or overheads in your office causes a false sense of security. Have another rehearsal in the room that you will be using; do not tempt the gremlins who lie in wait for trusting managers and staff members and cause havoc and distress when people are least able to cope. If the facility is not equipped with a screen, writing surface, easels, working microphone, and podium, rent or bring your own. If you have to lay a cord across the floor, make sure that you tape it down so that you do not create a hazard.

A come-to-your-aid kit that is replenished frequently and taken to every meeting is a wise investment. At the minimum, include:

- Extra projector bulbs
- Extension cords
- Different marking pens for paper and plastic boards; pencils
- Name tags
- Several varieties of tape and tacks
- Writing pads
- Scissors
- Aspirin

No environment is ideal. Now that you know its importance in the overall effectiveness of public meetings, choose the best available and take the time and effort to minimize or neutralize any negative effects or problems.

5

Making Effective Presentations

Will your meeting be congenial or confrontational? Comfortable or combative? Constructive or contentious? Does your group really value citizen opinion, or is the meeting just window dressing for decisions that have already been made? Whatever the meeting's purpose, well-organized and presented remarks set the proper tone.

Few people are born golden-tongued orators, but everyone can learn effective presenting skills. The rewards of a good performance, of knowing that you have reached out and spoken to the concerns of your audience, are immediate and satisfying. The reverse can be said of a mediocre or poor performance: you know, and the audience knows, and no one is satisfied.

This chapter discusses how to make individual and panel presentations as well as how to answer questions in any situation.

INDIVIDUAL PRESENTATIONS

The steps discussed below can be used by any busy professional faced with making a presentation. They presuppose—rightly, in most cases—that you have a wealth of information at your fingertips. Your challenge is knowing what and how much to say to each particular audience. You can be confident that you know more than most people about sewers, environmental protection, land use, social policy, transportation, parks, and any number of issues that are the subject of public meetings. And most audiences—elected or appointed officials as well as the lay public—need to know far less than the professionals, even when they make decisions. Each audience requires certain information at that time and that place, and your job as a presenter is to figure out what that is and give it to them—no more and no less.

Remember your purpose. The first step in organizing any presentation for a public meeting is to decide what the listeners need to know about the subject to give informed advice or make meaningful decisions. That depends in large part on the purpose of the meeting: is it informational, advisory, or decision making? If, for example, the matter is before a local planning board or commission, to help that body reach a decision, the staff presentation should provide an overview of the issues, options that can be considered, and recommendations for possible action. On the other hand, if the meeting is with a neighborhood group and thus probably for informational and advisory, not decision-making, purposes, the presentation should be less detailed than the one for the planning board, with ample time for questions and comments from the audience.

Know your audience. Organize your material only after you are sure of your purpose and have this information about the expected attendees:

- Number of people likely to come
- Average age and gender
- Occupation(s)
- General knowledge of subject
- Common opinions or biases
- Specific focus or special interests
- Known opposition to or support of the issues under discussion

Studies show that the attention span of the average American adult is two and one-half minutes—and decreasing all the time. If your presentation is more than 20 minutes long, help keep the audience's attention by choosing several speakers, using visuals to explain salient or difficult points, and scheduling ample time for questions. The latter is important to make sure that you deal with their issues, not ones you guess may be of interest.

In an early planning session, after you have decided the general areas of information that should be covered at the meeting and ascertained the likely focus of the audience, choose the most appropriate and credible spokespeople: those who can best convey this particular information to this particular audience. As discussed in

Chapter 1 on leadership, every meeting must have a convener or chair, someone who is indisputably in charge. If you are speaking to an organized group, its president or leader takes that responsibility. At your own meetings, the company president, agency director, or a political leader such as the mayor should take that role. These people are not expected to have definitive information about the subject at hand. Their primary responsibilities are to keep order and obtain and retain the respect and attention of the audience.

Similarly, as conveyers of information, the presenters do not have to possess the authority or the skills of the chair. They must, however, be able to convert complex or technical data into terms that a lay audience will understand. Graphics and audiovisuals can help, and there are a great variety from which to choose (see Chapter 6). But even the best cannot cover up the mistakes of a poor presenter.

> *The city manager knew that the proposal to widen the arterial street by removing 50-year-old trees would be controversial, so he asked the city's traffic engineering consultant to make the presentation at the public meeting, held at a local school. After being introduced, the consultant immediately darkened the room, turned on the slide projector, and began to speak in a flat voice. Never varying his tone, he took more than two hours to present all his slides, many of which were redundant, although he did show sound mitigation measures that could reverse the effects of the tree removal. There were about 75 people at the beginning of the meeting. After an hour, they began to slip out, and when the consultant finished, only 15 citizens were left.*
>
> *When the city manager called for public discussion and questions and there were none, he mistakenly surmised that the expert's presentation had mollified the opposition. On the contrary, they had been bored into submission—but only temporarily. The next day, angry citizens petitioned the city for a special meeting—not to hear any more information, they insisted, but to be heard themselves on this important issue. The consultant's presentation, while technically sound, was inappropriately long and tedious, and it unnecessarily alienated an important audience.*

Too many people in charge of organizations insist on making the major presentations at public meetings in the mistaken belief that only they have the appropriate credibility or status. Alas, as their staff people can attest after having to pick up the pieces, the top echelon may be the last people qualified for this task. Most often they are able generalists, not specialists; as such, they rarely know the fine points of the issues under discussion. It is best to leave the technical presentations to the professionals—insisting, of course, that they excise the jargon from their speech when talking to lay audiences.

Organize. Every presentation should contain no more than three major points. Professionals and technical experts often protest this important rule; they insist that they have 13 points, even 30, and that the audience must be apprised of all of them. But no audience is all-inclusive; each has its own special interests. In light of the above example of the street widening, consider my earlier admonition to organize presentations around what each particular audience needs to know. The adjacent neighborhood has different concerns than downtown businesspeople, who have interests different from senior citizens or the planning commission, and so on. By considering the audience first and adjusting your remarks to its needs, you can indeed find the three major points that interest these people. If the issue is a construction project, always include a time schedule, even if it is subject to change. That is the piece of information that citizens most often want to know and public officials most often want to avoid discussing.

After defining your audience and its needs, you may find that one presenter cannot cover all the material. If so, bring in others—but not any more than necessary, lest you risk repetition. Three presenters is usually a sufficient number: the first to give the introductory or broad perspective; the second, details; the third, more information or a summary. Each presenter should also be available to answer audience questions.

Build bridges with the audience with words such as *we, our,* and *us* rather than creating a gulf with *you* and *your.* It is important that citizens believe that you care about the issues as much as they do, even though you may disagree on specific points.

Help your listeners keep track of your presentation by using connectors such as these: "I'm going to cover three points today. The first is . . .," "Next, let's talk about . . .," or "That's one way to look at the issue. On the other hand . . ." Summarize at the end by repeating the most important points you want people to remember.

Use commonly understood short words and phrases and direct nouns and verbs. If you must use acronyms or jargon, explain it or provide a handout with a glossary.

Avoid jokes and humor directed at particular ethnic, racial, religious, or other interest groups. Such disrespect can be politically and personally damaging. On the other hand, do not be so stilted and formal that you cover up your genuine warmth and humanness. While public officials usually make poor stand-up comedians, they endear themselves to audiences when they tuck in appropriate anecdotes about themselves and their families and colleagues or appeal to people's pride and sense of fair play.

> *The local police chief began his remarks at a crowded neighborhood meeting by acknowledging his and the participants' shared concerns. "I understand your neighborhood's concern about adequate traffic control. My 10-year-old son crosses Logan Boulevard every day to go to school, and in our neighborhood we parents formed a safety patrol to try to slow down traffic in the morning." Later he commented, "We've all watched our city grow, and I'm proud that so far we've been able to work together to solve the tough issues."*

Never write your presentation word for word or you will read it word for word and sound mechanical and insincere, no matter how much you practice. It is better to outline your remarks, using visuals such as charts or graphs to help people follow along and to understand difficult concepts. Divide your presentation into a discernible introduction (what you are going to say, lightened up with an anecdote or two), body (those three cogent points we discussed earlier), and conclusion or summary (action or further steps needed). Keep the presentation short enough to fit easily into the time allotted.

Practice until perfect. It is important to schedule practice time as part of the pre-meeting planning schedule. After all the presenters have outlined their separate remarks, get everyone together and rehearse. If possible, include other staff members who know the audience or the subject but are not presenters. Despite your individual busy schedules, try to have at least two rehearsals, one several days before the meeting so that you have time to change the text or visuals and a dress rehearsal a day or a few hours before. Find time at a long coffee break, during a brown-bag lunch, before or after work—whenever everyone can get together. These dry runs are the only way you can be sure that all the important points are being covered, that no one is running over schedule, and that repetition has been eliminated. If the meeting room is unfamiliar, at least one person should visit it and report back before you rehearse. It is important to rehearse even if you are making a presentation in a familiar environment, however. Even when you know the setup, you still need to practice who is saying what, when, where you should stand or sit, and the best place for your audiovisuals.

During your rehearsal, have a frank discussion about what each of you will wear. Making sure you are dressed appropriately for the occasion and that you all do not wear the same "uniform" is not at all frivolous. People generally form their opinions about strangers in the first 30 seconds—before anyone says anything. Posture, demeanor, and dress are important nonverbal signals, and you want to send the right ones.

> *County engineers sponsored a series of meetings to talk to low- and moderate-income residents about a sewer system that the state environmental agency required the county to install within the next 10 years. The engineers were aware that this was not a popular subject, because the new sewer would raise everyone's property taxes. The meetings were for information only; citizens could not change the mandate. They could, however, express their opinions about the process.*
>
> *After the engineers rehearsed their remarks, they discussed what they should wear. They started by asking themselves what the particular audience expected county engineers to look like. They agreed that the dark suits, white shirts, and subdued ties that were standard dress for a meeting with downtown businesspeople were too formal and intimidating for an evening meeting in the suburbs. On the other hand, they felt that open-necked sport shirts and slacks would give the impression that they were too casual about such a serious subject. They decided rightly to wear sport coats, ties, and slacks. These engineers were all men, but women should have*

*had the same concerns and chosen suits or tailored dress-
es—no frills.*

Deal with stage fright. Even with the most meticulous preparation, most of us have some symptoms of stage fright before a presentation. Sweaty palms? Keep one hand in your pocket and out of
mischief, but make sure that you have no keys or coins that you can
jingle. The audience will never know that you have sticky hands or
a perspiring forehead unless you give it away by wiping profusely.
Dry throat? Avoid coffee, tea, colas, and other caffeine-laden beverages for several hours before; slake your thirst instead with cold
water. Squeaky voice? Citizens who have never seen you before
have not heard your normal voice, so never apologize or tell people
that you are nervous. Memory loss? Take a drink of cold water
(always keep a glass nearby), readjust your notes, look over the
audience knowingly, and repeat what you just said for added
emphasis. If all else fails and you still forget what comes next, summarize and finish up. The audience will never complain that your
presentation was too short.

The key points to remember about stage fright are that nearly
everyone has some of it sometimes, audience members cannot tell
that you are nervous unless you tell or show them, and knowing
your material and practicing will give you the confidence to overcome the worst of it.

Another way to give you added assurance to deal with stage
fright is to arrive at the meeting early. As was noted in other chapters, there are untold details at a public meeting that can go wrong.
You walk in at the last minute at your peril. Being early gives you
time to set up your audiovisuals, adjust the microphone to the
height and audio level you require, find and use the bathroom, and
become as comfortable as possible with the particular features of
the room. Being early has another advantage—you can meet and
greet the public as people arrive. Much as you may prefer to run
and hide from perceived enemies or critics, it is better to disarm
them by being at the door to shake their hands, engage in small talk,
and make it clear that you respect them and will be cordial and
polite—whatever your differences. Building rapport with as many
people as possible will give you unexpected friends and convince
others to give you the benefit of the doubt if matters become contentious. Keeping yourself busy will also deter you from becoming

nervous and tinkering with, and probably spoiling, your well-organized and rehearsed presentation.

PANEL PRESENTATIONS

Panel presentations, which allow for diversity of attitudes and expertise, can be very effective. The key players are the panelists and the moderator.

If you are a panelist at a public meeting, the same general rules apply to preparing and giving your remarks as apply when you are the sole speaker. Choose remarks appropriate to the audience, be organized, speak from notes instead of a prepared script, and adhere to the time schedule. Never be the one for whom the warning bell tolls, especially more than once. In addition, make sure that you know the following before organizing your panel speech: your specific topic, time allotted for each presenter, order and format, where you are to sit, and other logistics.

If you have a choice of position, volunteer to be either first or last. If you are a skillful lead speaker, your presentation can provide the framework for the entire discussion and, in effect, cause the others to respond. If you are last, you can be the summarizer and synthesizer, the one whose remarks are most likely to be remembered.

The other role is the often unheralded moderator, who must guide and organize the discussion while stimulating the audience to participate. Fulfilling this task without revealing your own opinions or prejudices and keeping the good will of all, is essential to the success of panel discussions.

Pamper panelists. The care and feeding of the discussants is a moderator's major responsibility. This includes arranging for any audiovisual equipment and a technician at least to stand by if anything goes wrong, making sure that there are sufficient handouts, testing the microphones, providing drinking water, seeing to it that the temperature and lighting in the room are comfortable, and doing everything else possible to make the presenters and audience comfortable.

Some moderators have the additional responsibility of choosing the participants on the panel. Giving due attention to gender, race, political affiliation, and other factors important to the issue and to the audience, moderators should choose participants who well represent the variety of interests concerned with the subject under discussion.

Effective moderators make every effort to confer with all the participants well before the day of the meeting, briefing them on the matters discussed above and encouraging them to summarize their remarks from careful notes rather than reading ponderous written documents. If a meeting of the entire panel is not possible, the moderator should arrange a conference telephone call so that everyone can review each other's outlines and note redundancies or gaps. The quality of the discussion is enhanced when everyone has the opportunity to rehearse and orchestrate needed changes beforehand.

> *"Listening to Florence just now, Jack, it sounds as if you're both saying the same thing, but no one is covering the issue of financing. Will you do that instead?" Or, "According to your summaries, you sound as if you all agree with each other, but the audience will want to know the differences. Who wants to take the opposite point of view?"*

The moderator should obtain a short biographical resume of each participant and make interesting, informative introductions that add credibility to each speaker.

Although everyone should come early, the moderator should be the first on the scene to check out the room and equipment, leaving ample time to take care of those last-minute problems that are sure to arise.

Make people comfortable. As noted in Chapter 4, the seating arrangement has a significant effect on the quality of any meeting. Arrange the room to facilitate discussion. For small groups—those of 25 or fewer, including panelists—arrange chairs so they all will sit around one large conference table or position several smaller tables in a U-shape, with moderator and panelists seated at the far end. By sitting furthest from the door, you ensure that latecomers do not disturb the flow of the meeting. A larger group may have to be seated in auditorium or classroom style, with the audience facing the presenters who are in the front of the room. This arrangement can inhibit free exchange unless the moderator actively encourages audience questions and participation. Even if you have sent a seating diagram to the hosts or janitorial staff, be prepared to have to rearrange things to suit your purposes—still another reason to come early.

Place identification cards in front of the panelists that spell their name and affiliation correctly in bold black ink. They must be large enough to be seen by everyone in the audience.

Do not skimp when ordering microphones. It is essential that all members of a large audience be able to hear all the speakers. Two people can usually share one tabletop mike comfortably, but three definitely make an awkward crowd. Clip-on or portable mikes are the most convenient, but disruptive if there is only one that has to be passed around among the panelists. In a small, informal setting, panelists may sit down when making their set remarks, though it is generally better to have them stand before a microphone and podium. They may sit when answering questions.

Moderators make presentations, too—albeit brief ones. In their opening remarks, they should welcome everyone; inform the audience where the bathrooms and telephones are located; review the purpose of the meeting, issues to be discussed, and schedule, including breaks and time for questions; and ask the audience to hold questions and comments until all the presentations have been made.

To avoid distracting bobbing and weaving, moderators should introduce themselves and all the panelists at the outset, stating names, credentials or affiliations, and general topics. Then, panelists can give their prepared remarks in turn without further introduction, following one another in the order in which they are sitting.

Keep on time. Moderators may give someone else the job of watching the clock, but they must not hesitate to cut off a presentation that is running well over its allotted time. Use prearranged hand signal cards to denote one minute, 30 seconds, and politely but firmly signal the speaker when the time is up. Stand up to give your message emphasis. If the speaker ignores your nonverbal sign and continues, with no end in sight, get tough. Stand near or at the microphone and say, for example, "Betty, I'm sorry, but I see by the clock that your 10 minutes are over. I know that you wouldn't want to cut into Bob's time." If for some reason you are nervous about controlling run-off-at-the-mouth speakers, bring along a loud alarm or timer and use it.

Even if the meeting is running on schedule, the moderator must be sensitive to the audience. If people are fidgeting, dozing off, talking to their neighbors, or showing other signs of boredom, call an unscheduled two-minute break or stretch-in-place.

QUESTION PERIOD

It is important to provide means for everyone in the audience, including those reticent to speak aloud, to ask questions. Sometimes, if there are many in attendance, this requires microphones at strategic locations on the floor where the audience is sitting. Other times, you may want to encourage written questions.

> *After the conclusion of panel presentations on the subject of U.S./Japanese sister-city relationships in the corporate offices of a prominent multinational company, the moderator asked for questions from the audience. Several Americans stood up and made comments, but after a few minutes it became obvious that none of the Asian guests was asking questions or remarking, even though they had been specifically invited to participate. The puzzled moderator called a short break and conferred with one of the Asian panelists, who informed him that Japanese were not accustomed to speaking out at public meetings. She suggested, however, that they might respond if written questions were invited.*
>
> *After the break, the moderator handed out cards, inviting audience members to write out their questions anonymously. He noted some of the Asian guests nodding and smiling. Soon afterward, several questions, some obviously from the Asian point of view, were submitted, and the dialogue became more inclusive.*

The moderator also is in charge during the question-and-answer period and should be prepared to start the discussion by asking a question of each participant or by "planting" questions among friends or colleagues in the audience. As noted above, if you are in a large room, there should be extra microphones for use by the audience. If they are not available, paraphrase or repeat each question so that everyone can hear.

Decide in advance whether it is necessary to ask questioners to state their name and affiliation and enforce whatever rule you make. There is no one correct way. If the proceedings are being recorded, it is probably important to know everyone's identity. On the other hand, you encourage more people to participate if they can choose to be anonymous. Accept only one question per person unless everyone has had a turn and there is time left.

Except on very formal occasions, it is important to set aside time after your presentations for questions, and for very good reasons. First, if the question-and-answer period is handled well, speakers have an opportunity to reaffirm their message. Second, they engender audience goodwill by giving people the opportunity to clear up ambiguities or uncertainties or state their own points of view. A well-structured question-and-answer session can go far in cementing the bonds of mutual understanding and respect, groundwork that should have been laid by the presenters with their original remarks.

If the question-and-answer time is disorganized, however, or if the speakers are rude, unprepared, or on the defensive, the good relations previously established with the audience are jeopardized. Prepare as seriously for the Q-and-A period as you do for your presentation. Make it the subject of one of your pre-meeting planning sessions, review the composition and expectations of your audience, and list the 10 most challenging questions people are likely to ask. If your planning group is not sure, consult with others who know the audience and its concerns. Then rehearse short, succinct answers to each question. To your subsequent surprise and delight, you will find that audiences rarely ask more difficult questions than you can devise.

> *County transportation department engineers held three public meetings to discuss a proposal to widen a heavily traveled roadway from two to four lanes. Starting with the same basic information, they tailored their remarks to each specific audience. The downtown businesspeople in the first group were interested in how the construction would affect access to their establishments as well as how much it would cost each of them. The next audience, older residents at a senior community center, wanted to know about how to control speeding on the street and whether the proposal would raise property taxes. The third, a preschool parents' group, was concerned primarily about children's safety but also about taxes. Knowing these concerns, the transportation engineers rehearsed questions that each group would likely ask, preparing themselves with financial information and a construction time schedule for the businesspeople, information about new pedestrian crossing lanes for the seniors, and so on. Forearmed, they were able to*

answer all the citizens' questions and concerns and to
appear credible and competent to each group.

Decide the following matters beforehand so that you are as organized for the Q-and-A as you are for your initial presentations. Who will call on the questioners? Answer most of the questions? Handle rude or unruly people? End the meeting? These roles should be assigned on the basis of ability, not because of hierarchical status. A strong chair can keep control of the meeting by fielding all the questions and assigning the most knowledgeable person to answer them, while a chair who is more of a figurehead should take a backseat and let the facilitator or presenter take charge.

It is important to prepare the audience beforehand by announcing when you will take questions, preferably after all the prepared remarks have been made. Send nonverbal signals to indicate a willingness to meet the audience on its terms. If you have been speaking behind a podium, stand to one side when you are answering questions. If you have been on a platform, move to the floor. A clip-on mike gives you more flexibility than a microphone on a stand.

Listen carefully to each question, nodding to indicate your attentiveness. You do not have to agree with what everyone says, but you must always respect each individual. Help the rest of the audience hear or understand fully by repeating or paraphrasing each query.

Be direct and honest, but take a tip from successful politicians: Do not fall for "red herrings" or baited questions. When someone says, "You just repeated the same old stuff that your staff report says. When are you going to get to the issues we're interested in?" You might answer, "If you'd like to see us include other items, we'd be glad to hear about them later; but first, as you can see by the agenda, we've promised to answer questions about the content of the report as you've heard it." Do not be belligerent or defensive.

Answer generically and avoid holding a conversation on an issue specific to only one individual or situation: "Please see me later to talk about our time schedule for construction on your street. But if the rest of you are interested, I'll take a minute to explain all the details that the state considers when we put together our construction schedules."

Generally avoid put-downs such as a brief yes, no, or maybe. Sometimes, however, one of these responses may be just the right answer to a long-winded question that is clearly out of bounds and annoying the audience as much as you.

Move off the bureaucratic pedestal by relating your answers to the audience: "Yes, I know how hard it is to know what's going on at city hall when we're open only when you're working. Let's see a show of hands. How many would come to an evening hearing?"

Show that you have been listening by agreeing with points that others have made. Never argue. Maintain your poise and composure despite the slings and arrows of discontented citizens and deal with contentious people with courtesy: "Well, ma'am, I understand your concern, but we'll just have to agree to disagree on this one."

Humor is a good way to relieve stress or tension, but only if it is in good taste and directed to the speaker, not the audience. Never tell a shopworn or off-color joke.

Some people come to public meetings just to make a statement, not to have their opinions changed. Hear them out, waiting patiently until they take a breath, which even the most long-winded surely will. Then cut in immediately: "Thank you. I see by the hands that many other people have questions to ask. Let's call on the man way in back." Avoid choosing someone close to the first speaker, because he may be a buddy who will back him up, in a similar long-winded fashion.

A sure way to risk losing the audience's goodwill is to try to force everyone to ask a question. Do not challenge a person who just wants to give a mini-speech by retorting impatiently, "Now that you've stated your opinion, will you please give us your question, sir?"

Be aware of and control your body language and nonverbal behavior. If you scowl while saying, "Yes, I understand," you contradict your words and appear insincere.

Never try to run away from a difficult question by referring it to staff or known experts in the audience unless you have their permission beforehand. At the very least, you risk further embarrassment for yourself as well as for the experts if they do not know the answer. On the other hand, do not hesitate to say that you do not know; then offer to obtain the answer as soon as possible. Ask questioners to give you their name, address, and phone number after the meeting. Do not waste everyone's time taking down that information during the meeting.

If you greeted people before the meeting and maintained an open and receptive demeanor when you made your presentation, you can take comfort in knowing that most of the audience is either neutral or on your side, unless you give people reason to turn against you by being rude and thoughtless during the Q-and-A period. Given the chance, an audience will often discipline its own rowdy members: "Come on, Phil, sit down. The rest of us want to hear what they have to say."

Stop the Q-and-A period three to five minutes before the scheduled conclusion of the meeting so that the chair or facilitator can make a quick summary. This is one of the most neglected but most important parts of any presentation. You, your staff, and the audience have been together for a while now, and people have most likely forgotten some or all of your major points. Tie things together before you adjourn: "We certainly have enjoyed being with you these last two hours. In summary, we would like to leave you with these three points: [the most important things you want them to remember]. Thank you."

Every public meeting should begin with one or more informational presentations, and every presentation needs to be carefully organized and crafted if it is to set the stage for the discussion that follows. Presenters, panelists, and moderators all play significant roles in assuring the success of public meetings.

6

Graphics and Audiovisuals

Generally, we remember about 20 percent of what we hear, 30 percent of what we see, and 50 percent of what we see and hear. Graphics and audiovisuals can help you increase the retention capability of your audience, but only if they are prepared carefully and used appropriately.

Too many managers allow staff members to rely on these techniques as the primary means of conveying their message rather than using them for what they do best—supplement, clarify, and reinforce verbal information. Even the best illustrations, by their very inanimate nature, are second best. Nothing can take the place of the most effective messenger—the human being who is prepared, articulate, and attuned to the audience. In fact, the wrong ones—or the speaker's use of the right techniques at the wrong time—can hinder even the best-prepared presentation.

> *It was 7:30 on a cold, wintry night. Though the 35 physicians, nurses, administrators, and citizen activists on the health futures advisory committee were eager to hear the highly touted consultant's remarks, they also were nervous about getting home before the predicted snowstorm made the roads impassable. He had been brought to town at considerable expense to give them the latest news of health care trends around the country and committee members were looking forward to talking with him about models they could adapt to their community's health care delivery system.*

Mr. Outside Expert was all business when he came to the podium; unloading a sheaf of papers from his briefcase, he asked that someone dim the lights. "I know you can't see this, but . . . ," he began, and proceeded to prove himself right. He clicked on an overhead projector and showed the first of many single-spaced, tightly printed pages from a book—his book! He soon made it very clear that all he had to say about health care he had already written. Assuming that no one in the audience had read his book, he proceeded to read whole paragraphs projected on the screen—page after page after page.

When Mr. Outside Expert was finally through with his reading lesson, the audience was half-asleep and too numb to ask but a few cursory questions. Besides, he had taken too long and their minds were on the long drive home. As they hurried out, disappointed committee members muttered that everyone's time and money would have been better spent had they just purchased 35 of his books and asked Mr. Outside Expert to stay home.

Many of us have endured—worse yet, some of us have perpetrated—such misuse of audiovisual equipment. However, proper audiovisuals properly used can help you show and tell about certain types of information more quickly and easily than just a verbal presentation. Most people today are accustomed to obtaining most of their information from the media, which distill it into 30- or 60-second TV or radio announcements and terse newspaper headlines accompanied by short stories and simple illustrations. We may bemoan the effect of all this on the American public's understanding of complex issues, but we would do well to master these techniques if we want to make successful presentations.

Graphs and charts that clearly illustrate technical concepts and processes or numerical comparisons can help a lay audience follow a complicated oral presentation and become the baseline for everyone's understanding and discussion. They have yet another value: in a contentious or controversial situation, skilled speakers can focus hostile questions on the graphics and explanatory material, thus directing anger and confusion away from themselves and toward a neutral entity.

Instead of using audiovisuals only at the beginning of a presentation, as most speakers tend to do, interject them midway as well, when the audience is getting sleepy or inattentive. Used that way, they can help you sum up the main points in a presentation or reinforce the audience's understanding of key points. Used again at the end, appropriate audiovisuals can make sure that everyone is still on track.

It takes real skill to be a humorous speaker without demeaning or poking fun at the audience, but a clever visual at the right time can do the job for you.

> *A professional planner in a major West Coast city intersperses his somewhat dry presentations with overhead transparencies of cartoons that illustrate situations familiar to his audiences. This technique has more than once defused a tense situation. As the people smile or laugh at the common foibles they see on the screen, they become more at ease with each other. The speaker is no less professional for showing that he does not take himself or his profession too seriously.*

Illustrations also can save time. Spoken words can be abbreviated if they are simple and clear. However, they should never be crammed so tightly with information that they themselves need lengthy explanation.

It stands to reason that no single technique suits every situation, and yet many people act as if it can. For example, staff members may become protective of charts, slides, or a video they have produced and overuse or use them inappropriately. At the pre-meeting planning sessions, after you know the purpose of your public meeting and have decided the content of each presentation, choose your graphics and audiovisuals by evaluating them in terms of these factors:

- *Purpose.* As noted above, illustrative material should complement, not overwhelm, your message. What is your reason for using them at this particular meeting? Would this audience be impressed with something slick and spendy, or are they more likely to find your message credible with a down-home and casual approach? There is a great variety, as you can see in the pages that follow.

- *Size of audience.* Chalkboards and charts have limited viewing range and thus do not communicate messages well to audiences of 50 or more; likewise, slides or videos may overwhelm a small group.
- *Visibility.* More than one speaker has set up the paraphernalia for a slide show only to realize too late that a third of the audience will be sitting behind pillars or posts without a clear view. Arrive early and position the screen, posters, or charts, then move through the room to check visibility. If visuals cannot be seen easily from all the seats, move the chairs or move your material, redo the visuals, or, if you are unable to change things adequately, go on without them. Audiences are forgiving if you explain why you have to give just an oral presentation, but they are unforgiving, and sometimes downright hostile, if all or most of them cannot see the illustrative materials.
- *Budget.* During your planning sessions, decide how much money you need and how much you can spend, and then choose the audiovisuals that meet those criteria. Clever graphic artists with more time than money can do wonders. But the cost definitely goes up, and the quality may go down, if you ask them to bail you out at the last minute.
- *Presenter's skill.* Never use a technique that is too complicated for the speaker to handle with ease. Hold a dress rehearsal that includes all the charts or boards you plan to use and practice standing to one side, not in front of them, when writing or pointing. Write legibly; if even your best handwriting is unreadable, enlist a helper to write for you, or have the writing done by a graphic artist ahead of time. If you know that you are apt to be especially nervous or are a klutz with even the most simple slide projector or video player, bring an assistant who can tinker quickly and successfully with balky machinery.
- *Message.* Suit the medium to the message, not the other way around.

The most commonly used graphics and audiovisuals are presented alphabetically in the pages that follow. The discussion of each includes advantages, disadvantages, and usage tips.

Table 6.1   Audiovisuals

Technique:	**Butcher Paper or Newsprint**
Advantages:	Inexpensive, portable, and disposable. May be preprinted with information the speaker wants to cover or used effectively to record ideas as they are expressed by either large or small groups. May be rolled up and taken back to the office for retyping in permanent form.
Disadvantages:	May appear too impermanent and frivolous for some formal occasions, such as hearings.
Usage Tips:	Always write firmly and clearly with dark-colored pens—no yellows, greens or oranges. Check out the host site beforehand. More than one presenter with a roll of preprinted butcher paper charts and a box of tacks has been thwarted by an adamant hotel manager who would not allow any holes in her expensive wall coverings. Masking tape sometimes can be used; find out the rules of the establishment well in advance so that you are not caught unaware.

Not having ascertained the rules beforehand, the public works director reluctantly admitted to a large audience, "We have these charts we want to show you but the hotel manager won't let us tack them on the walls. I'm sorry I didn't bring any tape. Can I have two volunteers to hold them up for me? We only have a dozen or so." Finding volunteers the same approximate height was one problem; getting them to hold their arms up for an hour without collapsing was another.

Technique:	**Computer Aided Maps, Charts, and Text**
Advantages:	Displays technical concepts visually and can be projected for viewing by large audiences. Allows presentations to be pre-programmed to integrate sound, photos, charts, tables, and text. Images can be reused on the Internet relatively easily for some one with basic computer skills.
Disadvantages:	Expensive and cumbersome, but price and size reductions can be expected over time. Some projection equipment may need to be rented. Requires a portable computer (laptop) or transfer of files between computers.
Usage Tips:	Keep text and graphics simple. More likely to have problems than less technical techniques.

Technique:	**Computer Aided Slides**
Advantages:	By pressing keys on a computer keypad, the speaker can project images that are more vivid and compelling than traditional slides.
Disadvantages:	Requires specific knowledge and considerable time and expense to set up. Malfunctions more often than other simple techniques.
Usage Tips:	Know your audience. Some may be impressed by the latest electronic gadgetry while others will be put off. Practice beforehand in the room you are presenting. As with all visual aids, design carefully to be clear and concise.

Technique:	**Chalkboards or Whiteboards**
Advantages:	Free if they come with the territory, as they usually do in schools and meeting or convention centers. Flexibility is the primary asset as words or ideas can be changed with the flick of an eraser or erasing fluid. The electronic whiteboard, on which text can be converted to a paper copy, is a high-tech and expensive version.
Disadvantages:	Not always available—particularly in hotel or church meeting rooms—and nearly impossible to rent or take with you. Clumsy. Impermanent; you will have to erase your previous words or arrange for a quick transcription if you run out of space. Limited visibility, especially white chalk on a scratched, dull, much-used surface. Most schools still have old-fashioned chalk or black boards and old-fashioned chalk, but too many of the boards are worn out and therefore hard to read. The schoolroom and pedagogical memories they evoke may be positive or negative, depending on your presentation skills and the background of the audience. The electronic version produces only one copy, useful for record-keeping, but minimal value in a discussion.
Usage Tips:	Whiteboards are much better than chalkboards—they are easier to read—but be sure you have the right kind of marker. Do not rely on your hosts to provide any equipment—not even marking pens.

Facilitating a workshop with elected officials whom she wanted to impress, the consultant picked up the colored pen that lay next to the whiteboard without looking at it closely. After she had written several lines, she attempted to erase her text and was embarrassed to find that she could not. She had grabbed the wrong pen—it was not "dry ink," the only suitable ink for whiteboards. This simple but obvious mistake made it much tougher for her to gain the confidence of the audience.

Technique:	**E-mail**
Advantages:	Inexpensive, ubiquitous, speedy, and disposable. A preferred method of communication for many people prior to and following a meeting.
Disadvantages:	Can be sent only to those who have e-mail addresses, less likely to be the poor and minorities. Organizers of public meetings may not have access to a sufficient number of e-mail addresses of all likely attendees. Should not be used as only means to communicate about a public event.
Usage Tips:	Write as clearly and succinctly as with all other techniques, avoiding abbreviations known only to a few insiders. Use the subject line to inform readers what the message is about and why they should pay attention.

Technique:	**Flip Charts**
Advantages:	Inexpensive, portable; you can easily bring your own rather than borrow one from the host site. Press-on letters may be used to enhance legibility. Ideas may be written down beforehand and then referred to as you speak of them. Like butcher paper, flip charts can convey your openness to new ideas and may encourage spontaneity and creativity, because they allow you to jot down ideas that arise from you or your audience.
Disadvantages:	Because they are so handy, flip charts are often misused. May not be seen clearly by the audience unless you use bold, strong, primary colors. Avoid yellow, which tends to fade out, and magenta, which people either love or hate. Small, scrawly writing also can be a visibility problem; if you cannot write legibly, have someone else do it, or practice until you can. For ease of viewing in the typical room, letters should be at least two inches high. Not a good visual aid in a large room. Check out the host site. If the flip chart cannot be seen easily from the back row, flip over to something else.
Usage Tips:	Clutter is the enemy of flipchart literacy, mainly because we expect too much from this medium. Write ideas or fragments, not complete sentences. But be sure to discuss or at least mention everything on the chart. If you skip over or ignore several points, you tempt the audience to fill in the blanks on its own, and the answers may not be the same as yours.

Technique:	**Geographic Information Systems (GIS)**
Advantages:	Opportunity to combine geographic and other data (e.g., demographics or values) to illustrate relationships and trends. Used by a growing number of public agencies and private firms. Results can be displayed on a printed map or computer presentation.
Disadvantages:	Expensive, though costs are decreasing. Requires specialized knowledge, equipment, and experience to use effectively. May be overkill for simple projects or displays.
Usage Tips:	For maps, determine the most appropriate scale, patterns, and explanatory information to communicate your message clearly. Keep relatively simple; do not try to communicate too much with a single graphic.

Technique:	**Graphs, Maps, Diagrams, and Charts**
Advantages:	Portable and flexible, if made beforehand on heavy, good-quality paper or posterboard that does not bend, tear, or wrinkle easily. More expensive than flimsy butcher paper or flip charts, but also more permanent.
Disadvantages:	Spoiled by the instant messages of the modern media, the attention span of most viewers is extremely limited, while at the same time, they expect high quality. Crowding in too many details and mediocre to poor lettering or duplication are pervasive problems. Too often done by technical experts without concern for the limited understanding of lay audiences.
Usage Tips:	Always check them out in the room in which they will be used, or, at the very least, know the size of the space and apportion them appropriately. Do not stint on quality of materials. Use bold colors. Make sure there is a surface to which they can be attached, or bring your own easels or room dividers.

With the availability of computer software programs for graphics, too many people who cannot draw a straight line think they can now be artists. Not so. The same rules for clarity, boldness, and simplicity apply as when we were all in the dark ages of pen and paper. Do not load your graphs, maps, diagrams, and charts with so much text that they require many minutes of observation or explanation. It is particularly important that your illustrations be self explanatory if they are viewed by an audience that is meandering about. Simple but complete legends or titles are matters typically overlooked.

Every map or photograph of a geographic area must have a north arrow; always include a standard title block that includes the name of the agency, department, the preparer (if an architectural or engineering firm, for example), and indication if this is part of a series ("Transportation Alternative 1, 2, 3, and so on"). If there is any chance that the managers of the facility will not let you mount the material on a wall, bring your own easels.

The city manager wanted good graphics for a series of budget presentations he was going to make throughout the community. To save time and money, he had his staff prepare only one set of illustrations and took it everywhere. Unfortunately, this approach was effective only some of the time. In some settings, such as grade school classrooms, the charts were too large and clumsy; in others, such as church meeting halls, they were too small. The credibility of the message and of the presenter suffered in both cases.

Technique:	Handouts
Advantages:	Help to avoid ambiguity or misunderstandings because you have something tangible to put in the hands of each member of the audience. Appropriate for: • Outline of your presentations • Important points you want people to remember • Copies of material you are projecting in overheads or slides • Charts, diagrams, and checklists • Articles from newspapers or magazines • Bibliography or related references • Glossary of technical terms
Disadvantages:	Primarily, high risk of sloppy product. In this era of state-of-the-art duplicating equipment, it is inexcusable to hand out anything that is messy or difficult to read. If your copying machine has broken down at the eleventh hour, take your material to a 24-hour-commercial printer. If you cannot rectify the problem, leave the handouts back at the office and make do without them, offering to send copies upon request.
Usage Tips:	There are two kinds: those you use as reference when you are speaking and those you want the audience to read later. Both must be prepared with careful attention to (1) format: use outlines, lists and short paragraphs; (2) attribution: make sure all material is printed on your agency's or organization's official stationery, or with the source neatly typed in one corner; (3) date and title: this is a pervasive omission, as obvious as it seems; (4) numbered pages: another common mistake is to leave pages unnumbered, probably because they were assembled from a variety of sources at the last minute; (5) quality of reproduction.

Never give out handouts beforehand, or you will be rewarded by seeing the audience, heads down, reading the material, instead of heads up, listening to your explanation. Do not insult the group by reading every word; instead, paraphrase and amplify the ideas on the written page. If your material is for reference only and you are not using it during your presentation, have it ready to be picked up afterwards. Always have enough so that each member of the audience can have one or more. If you run out, offer to mail copies to those you have slighted.

Technique:	Microphones
Advantages:	Permit speakers to project their voices without strain and thus to speak with ease to an audience of any size. Many people are not familiar with microphones and thus shy away from them when they should be used. If you are going to give many major presentations, learn how to speak into, regulate, and be thoroughly comfortable with the device. Speakers who think their booming delivery can be heard in a large room without amplification are usually mistaken and risk alienating people who cannot hear them.
Disadvantages:	As with anything else that aids your presentation, microphones can be a handicap if you are not familiar with them in general or if the one you are using is of inferior quality, emitting squeaks and static.
Usage Tips:	A microphone is a very sensitive instrument; it will pick up and amplify whispers and asides, coughs and paper shuffling—sounds you may not want the audience to hear. Nothing aggravates an audience more than being expected to read the lips of the speaker, however. If you cannot be heard well throughout the room, use a microphone. Test the mike beforehand. Never give the audience the impression that you are an amateur by waiting until everyone is seated and then banging on the mike forcibly to ask, "Can you folks back there hear?" Learn how to use the instrument just as you practice with any other audiovisual technique. Know how to turn it off and on. Adjust it to your height beforehand or take the time to adjust it just before you speak. If you move around during your presentation, ask for or rent a clip-on or portable microphone. If none is available, stay put.

Technique:	**Models**
Advantages:	A three-dimensional, to-scale version of proposed buildings, highways, or any major changes to the landscape can be more effective than one-dimensional drawings or maps. Citizens can walk around the model and get some sense of what the finished product will look like. A good model can be the centerpiece of an interesting oral presentation.
Disadvantages:	Expense is a substantial negative factor. Good models can cost thousands of dollars and require an expertise not usually found among professional or technical staff. Inflexibility is another disadvantage; once you have invested in an expensive model, there is often little you can do to make changes short of ordering another one. Depending on the size of the model, portability may be limited and only a few people can view it at one time.
Usage Tips:	Encourage citizen participation by investing in miniature moveable buildings, trees, cars and other components so that people can manipulate portions of the model. Mark streets and other landmarks clearly and distinctly.

Technique:	**Posters**
Advantages:	Portable and easy to mount, dismount, and remount; good posters can present the essence of a message simply and effectively.
Disadvantages:	May be moderately expensive if you have to hire outside artists or pay for printing a large quantity. Cannot communicate a complicated message, and may be considered too frivolous a medium for a serious project.
Usage Tips:	Be careful not to expect too much. Best as a vehicle for slogans ("Don't trash it. . . Recycle!") or bold, simple photographs or drawings.

Technique:	**Projected Media: Overheads and Transparencies**
Advantages:	Simple to prepare, do not require extraordinary artistic talent or technical know-how. Inexpensive transparencies can be made easily by drawing with a felt marker; computer drawings or more complicated illustrations can be reproduced on an office photocopier. Transparencies are flexible; you can change the order to suit the needs of specific presentations and uncover the information as you go along, thus controlling what the audience sees. You also can encourage audience participation by changing or erasing written text, or by starting with a blank transparency and recording people's ideas. Of all the projected media, overheads have two distinct advantages: you can face the audience when showing them, and they can be seen easily in a slightly darkened room, or better yet, under normal lighting conditions. Projectors are portable, if somewhat bulky, and not too costly either to own or rent. You may use any light-colored, blank wall to project your image, though a screen is always best.
Disadvantages:	May be overused just because of their advantages. Avoid the tendency to project closely printed lines of text. Keep your message simple and unambiguous. Transparencies can become dog-eared if used too often, but are easily and inexpensively remounted or replaced.
Usage Tips:	The most important investment you should make is in professional time to make projected media appealing and interesting. Never use anything with which you are not thoroughly familiar. An important caveat: If anything can go wrong, it most likely will go wrong—from power failures to burned out light bulbs and missing or too-short extension cords. Never read the image on the screen with your back to the audience. Facing them, use a pencil as a pointer, not a pen, as it may glint in the light. Follow the word or image directly on the transparency as it sits on the face of the projector. Always check your equipment in the room where you are giving your presentation. That will not ensure that no problems will arise as soon as your back is turned, but it will somewhat increase your chances of success. Practice how to position your material so that you can do it with the least distraction to the audience. Use examples to which they can relate. "These are overheads of sketches I made of Dresden taken on my last trip to Europe. If you use your imagination think of what we could do in our city," may make an audience wonder about how you could afford such an expensive junket instead of what you would like them to do—get ideas they can transfer to their town. Use all capital letters and triple spacing or larger print.

Technique:	**Projected Media: Slides**
Advantages:	Can convey feelings and images and capture people's imagination. Suitable for all sizes of audiences, but especially effective with large groups.
Disadvantages:	Requires a somewhat darkened room that invites the audience to doze, especially if the show is too long—10 to 15 minutes is the optimal length. There are more bad slide shows than good ones as too many presenters use the medium to overwhelm their audiences with redundant and boring images. Fancy artwork and graphics can substantially increase the cost and perhaps give the wrong impression, as some audiences may question this "unnecessary expenditure of public funds."
Usage Tips:	Experiment in the room beforehand and turn off as few lights as you absolutely need. Err on the side of having too few slides rather than too many. All lists should be succinct phrases, not whole sentences, leaving it to the presenter or narrator to fill in the details. Look closely at any photographs you want to use. Are they clear? Appropriate? Do they advance your message? A slide show may be simple and inexpensive or glitzy and costly, have its own sound track or be accompanied by someone reading a script. If the latter, make sure you have a microphone that works and a speaker who reads well and has rehearsed the technique of simultaneously flipping pages and changing slides. Be careful not to overwhelm audience members with Hollywood-type productions; they will be distracted from your message by their concerns about where you found the money to pay for the elaborate show. Gremlins breed in slide shows and can cause all manner of havoc. Never use one that is unfamiliar to you. Even if you have shown it many times, review it before each meeting unless you have locked it up in a vault in between. Remember that slides go in the tray upside down and backwards.

Technique:	**Video and Films**
Advantages:	Primary advantage can also be your downfall. In this age of sophisticated television and movie images, people are accustomed to getting most of their information and entertainment from the video or movie screen and readily accept this way of presenting ideas. The challenge is how to compete in quality with the slick commercial productions to which your audience is accustomed.
Disadvantages:	Cost and time are primary negative factors. Very few agencies can produce their own video or films and therefore must hire outside contractors.
Usage Tips:	Make sure the firm you hire can do more than put pretty images on the screen—it must know how to translate your information into terms people can understand. If you are a governmental agency on a budget, large companies, especially utilities, may have video or movie studios they will let you use; some may donate their equipment or personnel and make the production for you. In all cases, make sure you control the content. If you write your own slide or video script, remember that people hear words differently than when they read them. The script should mimic common speech patterns: short, concrete words and relatively simple sentence structure. It is far better not to use this medium at all if you cannot do it right. If you have the resources, however, either one can be a very effective carrier of your message.

Technique:	**Visual Simulation**
Advantages:	Helps laypeople understand the impacts of proposed physical change such as improvements to streets, sidewalks, or new developments. Images can be used on Internet web sites as well as at public meetings.
Disadvantages:	Expensive. Software is still improving.
Usage Tips:	Accompany with easy-to-understand written or oral explanations. Emphasize that these are some, but not the only, possible choices.

Technique:	**Web Page**
Advantages:	One of the best communication tools to reach people who are interested in the issue but may not be on any other mailing or contact list. Can be updated with some ease to include latest information or summary of meetings. May include simple questionnaire to obtain feedback from users.
Disadvantages:	Many people do not have access or do not know how to use. Must be well designed and written to capture attention. Somewhat expensive to use if single-purpose, e.g. not part of a jurisdiction's or organization's web page.
Usage Tips:	Should not be used as only means to communicate with the public. Must be graphically interesting to capture attention.

PRINCIPLES OF GRAPHICS AND AUDIOVISUAL USE

- Use audiovisuals to enhance, not replace, your oral presentation.
- Choose the right medium for the right audience, one that will make your message more clear or meaningful.
- Make them simple and unambiguous. If you have a considerable amount of information to convey, use several charts or slides rather than cram too much into one.
- In all lists, use phrases rather than complete sentences.
- Utilize a size and scale that can be seen easily by everyone in the room. Simple test: Hold your slide or overhead transparency at arm's length, up to the light. If you cannot read it with ease, your audience will not be able to see it either. Discard and replace with larger type.
- Choose strong colors—black or dark blue on white for charts, blues and greens for maps, with red or orange highlights on either. Avoid pastels.
- For projected media, paraphrase and augment written information; never duplicate pages from a text.
- Before using slides, check and double-check to make sure that they are in the right order, the right way up, locked in place. Always test them out in the actual room as close to performance time as possible.
- Bring your own equipment, including spare light bulbs, extension cords, marking pens, masking tape, and other necessities.
- Keep the room as light as possible—dim but not dark, giving your audience no opportunity to doze off without being noticed.

- Distribute handouts only when you need to refer to them, or give them to attendees as they leave.
- Face the audience, not the screen, chart, or whiteboard. Practice until you can write sideways with ease.
- On slides, transparencies, or charts, use the point of a pencil or your finger as a pointer. A human appendage is more friendly and less pedantic than a mechanical instrument such as a laser pointer.
- Show only those visuals that you need at the moment. If necessary, have a helper remove your charts or graphs as you finish with them.
- If you have any doubt about whether you can be heard, use a microphone.
- If anything goes wrong, do not apologize or fiddle unduly with the machinery. You should know your subject well enough to extemporize when necessary.
- Remember that one picture is indeed worth a thousand words, but only if it is the right picture!

7

Dealing with Attendees at Meetings

Everyone who has a stake in the outcome of a meeting tries to promote an agenda and most of this book discusses how the managers and organizers can have a successful event. We should not be surprised, however, when members of the public represent a special interest or express points of view that are contrary to our own or appear to challenge our leadership. Thoughtful, enthusiastic, and vocal attendees, even if they tend to get off the track we have laid so carefully, should not be considered barriers to successful meetings. Chairpeople, facilitators, and discussion leaders can deal with problem situations if they maintain a sense of humor, show goodwill, and adhere to the democratic process.

The common and uncommon difficult ones, and ways to deal with them, are discussed alphabetically below. It is important to note that most people are cooperative and want to work with you to have a successful meeting. Among those who are not we find the following:

Accusers. "I've been listening to you for 20 minutes now, and it's the same stuff you bureaucrats always say. You don't want to hear from us citizens. You'll just go and do what you want anyway." Accusers are often arguers gone amok. The first step in dealing effectively with them is to make sure their accusations are not correct. If accusers are right, you have no recourse except to promise to mend your ways. If you have truth on your side, several techniques can defuse them. Answer patiently, but not patronizingly, "Sir, I can understand your frustration; I've been to meetings like that too. But I can assure you that this time we're listening and will take everyone's comments into consideration." Then follow up your words with action: "Charles over there is tape recording everything being said at the meeting, and we'll go over the tapes afterward. If you want to add to your comments, please give us written suggestions before you leave."

Diffuse the accuser's anger by requesting a positive contribution: "Let's review what we've discussed already. If we haven't included your concerns, you're welcome to restate them for us." Resist the impulse to answer in the same tone of voice. If accusers have been to many public meetings, they probably have some cause for skepticism.

Apathetics. "I'm not really interested in being here. My spouse (or boss or neighbor) nagged me, so I tagged along." Disgruntled apathetics do not have to say anything to reveal their feelings. Just watch their body language: They tilt back in their chairs, arms across the chest in a show-me attitude, drum fingers on the table, fidget, and look everywhere but at the speaker or discussion leader. In a large gathering, this behavior and attitude affect only those immediately near the apathetics and usually can be ignored by the chair; not so in a small group, where they can disrupt the flow of discussion. Instead of allowing apathetics to sit outside the group (thus reinforcing their count-me-out attitude), welcome them into the circle: "I'm sure that we can make room for one more; it's important that we hear from everyone."

Challenge their harmless but restless natures by engaging their particular interests: "Jill, you were in Costa Rica last year. How does their literacy rate compare to ours?" Or ask them to take on a neutral task that will get them involved: "Would you make sure that everyone turns in a questionnaire after our discussion?" If all efforts fail to engage them, keep a watchful eye out to make sure that the insidious virus of their behavior does not affect others.

Apple-polishers. Some folks have not changed since grade school. Back then, they were always trying to be teacher's pet by giving the answer they thought was expected or jumping up to do favors. In the adult world, they still try hard to please the person in authority. Though they may have become more subtle, they give themselves away by their undiscriminating deference to the leader: "Joe's in charge, and as far as I'm concerned, whatever he says goes." Much as it may please your ego, that attitude puts too much of a burden on the leader and is not in the interest of good group dynamics. It is nice to be complimented on a new shirt or outfit, but on your shoes and haircut, too?

Be wary of fawning and false flattery and be suspicious of a possible hidden agenda. Answer the compliment with a simple thank you and then keep things moving by asking a direct question to the entire group. "What three priorities should we recommend to the City Council?" Apple-polishers can be persistent, and they may make other members of the group feel hostile if they appear to be succeeding in gaining the leader's favor. If you do not succumb, you will earn the respect and gratitude of the people who count— the rest of the participants.

Arguers. Some of this type start out with a smile and a disarming, self-deprecating remark such as, "Well, I know this is only my opinion, but. . ." That preface is the last time the arguer will be modest. If allowed to continue unchecked, arguers will make it clear that they value their right to state their points of view more than they want to hear from anyone else. They speak loudly and authoritatively from an arsenal overloaded with gossip, hearsay, innuendo, and sarcasm. Listen politely the first time, or even the second, lest you be accused of not giving them the respect they or the group think they deserve. But take control soon. Neither argue back nor ask a question that invites them to continue the discussion and discourages others from participating. Remember, it takes two to argue. Your reasoned response and fair-handedness will wear down the most determined arguer.

Attackers. A mentally or physically abusive bully may target the chair, a presenter, or even someone in the audience. If you are being attacked verbally, the old adage, "Sticks and stones may break my bones but names will never harm me," may give you some comfort. Try not to take the assault personally. Attackers are most likely angry not at you but at the system, the organization you represent, or perhaps even a lazy bum brother-in-law who works somewhere in the system.

Attackers usually speak hurriedly and in a loud voice. Resist the tendency to answer in the same hostile tone and accusatory language. Put them off guard by slowing down the momentum and answering deliberately, in a modulated tone. Emphasize a particular point that you know has the concurrence of most of the group or will focus everyone's attention back on the agenda: "Yes, ma'am, it's obvious that you feel strongly about this issue, but it's already

8:30 and we promised to finish the other items on the agenda before we adjourn at nine. Why don't we take up everything else now? We'd be glad to stay and talk with you afterward."

Another effective technique for cooling off attackers and the heat that they generate is to call a short recess. Take that opportunity to confer with your colleagues or friendly members of the audience, involving them in a strategy for dealing with attackers and depriving them of their primary weapon: the us-versus-them ploy that pits you against the public. But avoid an ill-timed or overly long recess that allows attackers to marshal their forces and put you on the defensive.

On rare occasions you or your staff may actually be attacked physically. If you are forewarned and the threat is serious, arrange for protection. Plainclothes guards are less intimidating to the audience than uniformed police, but if the uproar gets out of hand at the meeting, you may have to call the police anyway. Alternatively, you could adjourn the meeting; but realize that you are only deferring, not solving, the problem.

Some elected officials seem to enjoy verbally abusing staff members who are making oral presentations. If you are the hapless target and you want to keep your job, maintain your professional demeanor; do not fight back, then or later. Most likely you are the scapegoat for a political purpose—perhaps the official is trying to get reelected by pandering to a particular constituency—that has little or nothing to do with you personally.

Bashfuls. Truly bashful people have little self-confidence and do not believe that they have anything to contribute; thus, they rarely volunteer their opinions. Do not embarrass such individuals by seeming to pick on or talk down to them: "Well, Jane, you've been quiet as a mouse all evening. Come on, now. What's your opinion?" An effective way to bring them around, one that works best with no more than 15 or 20 participants, is to invoke an inclusive process that involves the whole group. Go around the table and ask each one in turn to answer a specific question: "If you could think of one word to describe our community, what would it be?" Bashful types can thus participate without being singled out. Another way to involve them is by catering to their shy, retiring natures: appoint them recorders. They are often accurate, thoughtful, and articulate as long as they do not have to speak out loud.

Chip-on-the-shoulders. These people are habitually resentful and angry, daring everyone to insult or injure them wherever they go, not just at your meeting. Those who know them are wary or even hostile, and generally not very forbearing: "Come off it, Harry. No one said you were at fault." As the leader, you can kill them with kindness. Give them credit for even the most insignificant contribution, implying that they have no excuse for acting like the injured party.

Dominators. There are two kinds of dominators—those who know nothing and just want to boss other people around and others who know too much and are impatient with any deliberative process. Their outward behavior is similar: They try to monopolize the discussion, present their opinions forcefully, and intimidate the more reticent members of the group. Dominators do not wait very long to show their colors. If you have seen them in action beforehand and find them part of your group, head them off early: "I know that you have strong opinions about this, Stephanie. Why don't we start off by taking a minute for you to tell us what you think the issues are?" After she pontificates for her allotted time, you can cut her off with impunity by turning to others.

Though dominators seem to run on incessantly, they have to breathe eventually. When they stop to take that breath, be alert. Seize the opportunity to interrupt or redirect the discussion. If these benign methods fail, simply ignore the dominators. They are used to this treatment.

Doubters. "I don't see how this can work. It never has before." Doubters are incurable skeptics; they cannot bring themselves to believe that anything good can happen that they did not personally observe or invent. They often accompany their negative remarks by nonverbal behavior, such as scowling, knitting their brows, or shaking their heads vigorously. If they are allowed to monopolize the discussion, they may have a negative influence over others.

Take control by suggesting that the group first hear everyone's ideas without discussion or evaluation. When doubters start their down-in-the-mouth comments, you can refer to the rules: "Remember? We said we wouldn't prejudge anything. Let's hear what everyone thinks." Be positive: "I can understand why you feel that way, but with all the good minds around this table, I'm sure we can figure out how to work out our problems." After enough of this positive reinforcement, most dyed-in-the-wool doubters will hear an idea they can support.

Dropouts. Slumping in their seats in the back of the room or off to the side, dropouts yawn, doodle, look out the window, or conspicuously read something entirely irrelevant to the subject of the meeting. The leader needs to make a quick assessment about whether to try to win them over or ignore them. Consider several factors: whether the dropouts always behave this way or are bored just with this issue, whether their inattention will infect the others, and whether they will have anything constructive to say if cajoled into being part of the group. In other words, is it worth diverting time and attention from the others to court them?

The dropouts' negative attitudes are often directed not toward you but toward the subject ("I thought this meeting on zoning was a real estate seminar"), their companions ("My friends made me come"), or even indigestion ("My stomach hurts"). If there is a break, you may want to seek out the dropouts to see if anything reasonable can be done to engage their attention. Benign neglect may be your best recourse, however, because they are generally too lazy to convince others to drop out with them.

Eager beavers. Some people are so anxious to be liked and to be part of the group that they seize on any or all ideas without giving them much thought. One might say, "I really agree with Joan. We should put all our money into a new park," only to back a completely contrary point of view just a few minutes later. "Wow, Jack's right! Let's spend all our money on a good, old-fashioned street fair." Eager beavers are too flighty to be good leaders, but they can be valuable at backing up whatever course of action the group embarks on. Hear them out politely, but do not expect them to be bellwethers.

Fence-sitters. Like eager beavers, fence-sitters have few opinions of their own. They are reluctant to say anything, however, until they see where the majority, or the people with the most status or influence, are going. Fence-sitters figuratively—or sometimes literally— look to the right and to the left to see where the opinion wind is blowing before they commit themselves. They also equivocate: "It seems to me that Mary is right when she says that we need a budget increase, but Jerry is also right when he says that we need to rein in expenditures."

Fence-sitters can contribute to a discussion when you need balance, but they are ineffective in a partisan argument and in helping the group come to a conclusion. It does no good to become impatient with them or try to force them to make a premature decision or recommendation. Do not expect them to leap off that fence until it suits them. You may have to ask the group to vote in order to force fence-sitters to make a decision.

Gossip-spreaders. "Well, I didn't hear it firsthand, but. . ." Gossip-spreaders enjoy the attention they receive when they disrupt meetings with hearsay that has little or no basis in fact. Their voices sound authoritative, but their words are vague and indefinite. They throw out just enough information to tantalize people or stimulate their imaginations so that other are encouraged to add their own tidbits. If you think that someone else may have more or correct information, call for it: "Has anyone else heard the mayor say he'll fire the city manager?"

If no one can refute the gossip-spreader, but you know that the group is getting off track, enlist everyone in finding a solution. "Does anyone know how we can find out what's really going on?" Call a short break. If the gossip-spreader's snippet makes no difference to the discussion, do not refer to it again when you reconvene. Gossip-spreaders thrive on the fact that nearly everyone enjoys talking about someone else.

Hair-splitters. Usually accountants, attorneys, scientists, or computer wizards who are well paid on the job to dissect data, hair-splitters do not understand that the same positive attributes that serve them well in their professions can discourage free-flowing public discussion. They contribute well when talking about the city budget but less effectively when discussing such nonquantifiable subjects as community values. Assign them the role of recorder or secretary and they will be so conscientious about watching over the accuracy of what everyone else says they will not have time to split hairs themselves.

Jump-ups. Excitable, enthusiastic, high-energy cheerleaders who are more interested in style than substance and have no patience with deliberate thinkers, jump-ups can be catalysts for getting a slow group going. They also may engender hostility, however, especially if they interrupt too often (as if their ideas were the only ones worth noting). Do not call on jump-ups for their opinions; you will hear from them soon enough. Turn to others for substantive discussion. Do not make them recorders or summarizers, either, because their handwriting is often as nervous-looking as they are; furthermore, they may write down only their own ideas.

Know-it-alls. "I've lived in this town since before many of you were born, and let me tell you, those new ideas will never work." Or, "I'm a registered engineer, and I know that you can't build a sewer system that way." By the law of averages, know-it-alls are right some of the time, and sometimes they are half-right. Most often, however, they are noisy interrupters who will disrupt the group process if you let them. Acknowledge their expertise only if it applies specifically to this situation. "Yes, it's really helpful to have an engineer with your knowledge of sewers, but even those of us without a technical background need to have a say about how we want to pay for them."

If their credentials do not apply, say so: "I understand your field is electronics. I'm not sure how that relates to sewers. The civil engineers who've studied this project tell us it's feasible." If know-it-alls continue their rude behavior, encourage the group (which does not like them any more than you do) to discipline them. "I hope you'll admit, Bernie, that all citizens are entitled to help make this decision."

Laggards. Whereas dropouts generally find a seat quietly in back, laggards amble in late and move to the front—visibly and often audibly—stepping over and around anyone in their way. Their haughty manner indicates that they think the meeting should begin when they arrive. They try to interrupt the proceedings by asking a question to enable them to catch up: "I know you may have covered this already, but . . . "

As the leader confronted with chronic laggards, do not show your displeasure with a scowl. They will not notice, and the rest of the group may be offended. Still, you need not put up with persistent interruptions. Offer to meet them at the break or after the meeting to fill them in. "We have a tight agenda, and I know the rest of you want to move right along." If you always start on time, laggards will realize that when you are in charge, they miss important parts of the meeting by being chronically late.

Sneak-outers. People who come on time but rudely disrupt the continuity or momentum of a meeting by leaving abruptly, usually without an explanation, may really have an emergency. Most times, however, they are registering a nonverbal protest against the subject, the format, or the organizers of the meeting. Some, of course, just lack manners. Whatever their motives, the group leader must not legitimize their behavior.

Spying a sneak-outer, one inexperienced moderator interrupted her presentation with an inept attempt at humor: "Oh no, Patricia's leaving. She's really going to miss something. We should have locked the door so she couldn't get out early." She thus called attention to behavior that half the group had not noticed—and the sneak-outer sneaked out anyway.

Discourage this behavior by suggesting a contract with the participants at the beginning of the meeting: "According to our agenda, we're going to have a two-hour meeting. Is there anyone who has to leave early?" Deprived of their primary weapon—the element of surprise—sneak-outers just might stay put.

Stand-patters. Do not waste your time trying to confuse some people with the facts; they have their own stubborn opinions and will not budge. Stand-patters are rarely interested in anyone else's point of view; even documentary evidence will not convince them. "So what if those radicals say that the river is polluted. When I was a kid we never had a fancy pool at the high school. If the old swimming hole was good enough for us, it should be good enough today."

Sometimes stand-patters' obstinacy can have a positive effect by causing the other group members to think through their opinions and defend them with facts and figures. As the leader, you must give stand-patters time to state their case, but when it becomes obvious that their opinions are not shared by the others, move on, politely but firmly.

Single-issuers. Whatever the stated agenda, some people come to all meetings with the same point of view. If group members know these single-issuers from past experience, they will smile indulgently while listening to their spiel and then go on about the real business of the meeting. Even if no one has seen them before, they give themselves away soon enough by their persistent narrow-mindedness and disinterest in topics other than their own. These people are usually harmless and just want to be heard.

Let the single-issuers speak—once—but do not respond if they are way off target. Quickly direct your attention to getting the meeting back on the agenda. Sometimes the only way to keep single-issuers out of mischief is to appoint them to a subcommittee—of one. "Jason, no one else seems to be interested in the life cycle of the beetle, so why don't you look it up and get back to us?" With any luck, he will miss your next meeting because of another, where he is more assured of a sympathetic audience.

Talkers. Many meetings are attended by at least one person who pontificates too much, too loudly, and too long. Like stand-patters, they are opinionated, but they have an added obnoxious characteristic: overbearing attitudes. Though they blurt out opinions without discretion, they expect to be taken seriously on everything they say.

If a talker has status with the group—is the president of the organization, or the mayor, for example—you may have to put up with their speeches. Call a short break and take the talker aside, asking, "Am I in error in thinking that an important goal of the meeting is to get other people's opinions in addition to our own?" The talker probably will understand your message and quiet down.

If the talker is not a VIP who must be catered to, take more direct action. Overcome your natural tendency to move away and actually get closer. This is especially effective if the talker is seated. Stand up close, wait for the talker to take a breath, and say, politely but firmly, "Thank you"—nothing more. Then redirect the discussion to the subject at hand and turn to the others in the group. Summarize what the talker said only if it is relevant to the discussion.

Walkers. Sometimes people pace at length around the room, and there is little you can do to stop them. Other walkers leave the meeting at an inappropriate time. Like sneak-outers, they want to call attention to themselves, but they do so with a flourish. Stomping from the scene, they may exclaim, "I can't stand anymore of this." The silent treatment is best. Walkers lose status and credibility as soon as they run away.

Groupies. The behavior of groups as well as individuals can present a challenge to leaders of a meeting. People who come to the meeting as a clique often make sure that they are noticed by waving placards or posters, yelling and shouting, marching and demonstrating. They hope that by showing strength and cohesiveness, they can intimidate the sponsors and disrupt the proceedings. They often are more interested in calling attention to their cause, especially if the media are present, than in influencing others to join them or even in affecting the outcome of the proceedings.

In the heat of battle, it may seem that they speak for the majority, but despite their organized ferocity, they are usually a minority and should be treated as such.

> *More than 100 people came to a community meeting to talk about alternative ways to finance the public school system. They picked up their numbered name tags*

and information packets and gathered around the refreshment table. The organizers were surprised and delighted at the large turnout and looked forward to a spirited discussion. Just before the meeting began, a group of people entered, obviously together. Carrying handmade placards declaring, "No new taxes," they started to organize a demonstration.

The five-foot-two chair walked over to the six-foot-two leader. "Thank you for coming, sir; I hope that you and your friends will all go to your numbered tables. We're just about ready to begin, and we only have two hours to cover a lot of ground." Expecting to be treated rudely, he was taken aback by her politeness. "Well," he sputtered, "we don't want a sales tax rammed down our throats, and we want to make sure that everyone knows it." "I understand," she answered. "Why don't you put your signs up against the wall? That way everyone can see them, but you'll be able to participate in the meeting." He reluctantly told his followers to lower their signs and play by the rules. "Okay, I can see that you really mean business," he said.

The chairperson's cordial but no-nonsense approach defused a potentially unpleasant scene and won plaudits from the more reasonable members of the audience, who were in a clear majority.

When dealing with groups of people, just as with individuals, it is important to remain even-tempered. When they shout, speak in a moderate tone. When they talk rapidly, respond slowly and deliberately. If there is time, the chair may give them five minutes or so to state their views. But in giving, the chair retains the authority to take away, and that prerogative must be made clear.

If a group disruption occurs during the presentation part of the meeting and the audience becomes noticeably restless, call a short break and then move on to the discussion phase. In that way, you remove any chance for them to take over the meeting. Remember that the majority in the audience is reasonable and will back you if you are fair and remain in control.

The very nature of a public meeting—a place where human beings interact and controversial issues are discussed—is fertile territory for all manner of people with distinct personalities and points of view. The alert leader acts to minimize or neutralize the problems, knowing that the majority will be grateful for such decisiveness.

8

Positive Media Relations

Many managers and executives are convinced that anyone connect-
ed with the media is a pest, a nemesis, an adversary—or, at best, a
necessary evil. In their opinion, the media intrude upon their private and public lives by asking unwarranted and unwanted questions, distorting the truth, following their own agendas, and generally impeding rather than fostering positive relationships.

On the other hand, the media see themselves as guardians of the
people's right to know and the conveyers of truth and information
that otherwise would be hidden or at least obscured.

There are abundant examples supporting both points of view,
though the truth most often lies somewhere in between. But the
facts of present day public life cannot be denied: The media are here
to stay, and all those who plan and direct public meetings ignore
them at their peril. Moreover, whatever their faults, the media are
not part of a monolithic conspiracy plotting to trap the unwary.
They are separate and extremely competitive businesses whose
practitioners take their jobs seriously.

PRINT, RADIO, AND TELEVISION

To deal with the media effectively, it is important, first, to recognize
their distinct characteristics. Just as there is an obvious physical difference between print and television and between television and
radio, so are there distinct differences in their modes of operation.

Next, accept the fact that media representatives are generalists;
you are the specialists. In most cases, you and your staff know more
than they on the subjects you want them to cover. You cannot expect
accurate or thorough reporting if you do not distill that information

into a form the media can understand. Make sure your media releases are clear and comprehensible, and you are more likely to receive the attention that you think you desire. In one short paragraph, present the essence of your message. If you are announcing a meeting, describe what will happen if the report/recommendation/project that is the subject of the meeting is accepted. What will happen if it is not? What will be the effect on the schools, seniors, local economy, quality of life, or any other factors of importance?

Successful relations with the media are never one way, and those executives who try to "manage" the news rarely succeed for long.

> *The nervous secretary interrupts the harried city manager's staff meeting to say that a local television reporter is on the phone. When he reluctantly takes the call, the reporter says, "We understand that you've found a major ring of thieves inside city hall—employees who have stolen thousands of dollars of valuable equipment in the last eight months. I'll be right over with a camera to find out what you intend to do about it." The city manager is noticeably upset. He stutters as he objects, "Well, we weren't going to release that to the public until tomorrow night, when we have our regular city council meeting. We still have some loose ends to tie up." The reporter is persistent, citing the public's right to know—now. The city manager reluctantly agrees to see the reporter in 15 minutes, leaving himself barely enough time to gulp down a cup of coffee with two aspirin.*
>
> *The interview does not go well; the reporter implies that there is a cover-up, and the city manager feels trapped, saying much more than he should. That evening he is dismayed to hear the local television news anchor— who, by the way, was not the person who interviewed him—begin the program with, "In an exclusive interview today, the city manager reluctantly revealed to our news staff that there is a major theft scandal at city hall. Is this a cover-up? Well, you judge for yourselves."*

When faced with forceful, pushy media representatives, even individuals accustomed to making decisions and being in charge let the media control them. In this case, the city manager—surprised and dismayed that news of the alleged theft had leaked out before the public meeting—still did not have to grant the media interview immediately. He could have said, "I'm sorry, but I have an urgent appointment now. I'll be glad to see you in two hours." Delay for good reasons is acceptable. Stonewalling—"I can't give you any information," or "No comment"—is not. It raises a red flag to the media and gives the impression that you have something to hide. The city manager had every right to give himself a little time to collect his thoughts, review pertinent material, and ask principals in the investigation to join him in the interview.

Even if the intrusive reporter and camera person had appeared on the city manager's doorstep, he could have asked them to wait at least as long as it took to catch his breath and get the staff he needed to back him up. Then he could have held the keys to a successful media interview, controlling as many factors as possible and maintaining poise when matters threaten to get out of hand.

Before any media encounter—whether on the phone, on the scene, or in the studio—ask reporters what they want to talk about. This gives you a chance to decide generally what you will say and how you will say it. If you are interviewed over the phone and are particularly apprehensive that you may get rattled and not say exactly what you want to, jot down an outline. Notes will help you stay on track, and no one but you can see them. If you have successfully stalled for time, fulfill your end of the bargain by returning the phone call or being available for the personal interview when you promised.

An effective manager is willing to share the glory as well as the blame—and certainly the responsibility—whenever possible. To reinforce your reliability and responsiveness, bring in everyone else involved: elected officials, staff people, consultants on whose reports you are relying. If only briefly beforehand, talk it over to make sure that you know what each of you will say. Try for a consistent, clear message.

Whenever possible, hold the interview in your office, on other familiar turf, or on a site of your choice that illustrates the issue well. In other words, control the territory. A television studio is the least friendly and most intimidating setting. As discussed in the section about television, these negative factors can be overcome; but whenever possible, be proactive. If, for example, you are talking to reporters about open public forums to discuss the state's fiscal crisis, your message will be most effectively conveyed if you are photographed in your office, at your desk. You want to be surrounded by trappings that send the message that this public servant is working diligently on a serious problem. On the other hand, if you are being interviewed about neighborhood meetings to discuss your community's new mandatory recycling program, invite the media out to the landfill and use the mass of solid waste as the backdrop to reinforce your message. Whenever you can, create photographic opportunities, and you are likely to receive more satisfactory television and newspaper coverage.

Learn a lesson from astute politicians: Never fall for baited or leading questions. The city manager in the earlier example could have blunted the reporter's sensationalist tone by putting the matter into perspective: "Yes, we certainly are concerned when anything is stolen from the city. But I think it's important to note that the value of what we lost is about $3,000. Though that's significant, we have $2 million worth of office equipment safe and sound." Or he could have challenged the reporter's assumption of a conspiracy: "That's not my information. Where did you get the idea that hundreds of items have been stolen?"

A primary reason that professional and technical people are often misquoted, or dismayed when they see how they are treated by the media, is because they are not accustomed to speaking in headlines or "sound bites." Be quotable by avoiding long and complicated sentences. Distill your message into five or 10 words, in simple English, and you will be pleasantly surprised at how often you are quoted directly and completely.

On the other hand, do not be reluctant to say those three little words, "I don't know," as long as you add, "I'll get the information for you." Do not pretend to be the expert on everything, but volunteer to help the reporter find out or assign a staff person to get on it immediately. There may be times when you cannot tell everything you know, but you should never tell an untruth.

Never say anything that you do not want repeated in the media. Even if you insist that something is off the record, reporters—while honoring your confidence—may validate what you have said with others and then repeat the substance without attributing it to you.

A good way to help ensure that the media understand your point of view is to summarize at the end of the interview, reiterating the points that you have made and asking reporters if they have any

additional issues to discuss or clarify. Still, you can never completely control how a story is reported, and you should not try to. Never
ask to review the reporter's story before it is printed, for example.
You will certainly be rebuffed and perhaps resented for wanting this
unwarranted control.

There are many ways to be proactive in obtaining the attention of
the media, and through them, the public.

REACHING OUT

An effective approach, though one not often used by busy organizations because it takes time, is to stage an event. As was noted previously, the media are more likely to attend an interview or
announcement if you hold it at an interesting and photogenic location; likewise, the public interest is aroused more readily when you
go "on location." Try to share the spotlight with sure-fire subjects,
such as children, pets, or the elderly. If you are holding a public
forum on children's safety, for example, announce it on a play-
ground or near a particularly dangerous school crossing. Invite concerned parents, teachers, and children, and be sure that they get in
any picture. Or sponsor an essay contest on the subject and
announce the winners at their schools, all the while calling attention
to the scheduled public meetings on the subject. Want to get the
word out about a public meeting to discuss regulating nursing
homes? Invite the media to an appropriate facility—preferably one
that meets your criteria rather than a bad example, unless you really want to stir up controversy.

In certain situations, public service announcements (PSAs) are
useful. In the not-too-distant past, radio and television stations were
required to provide a certain amount of time in the public interest
in order to keep their Federal Communications Commission licens-
es. This is no longer the case, and many stations are reluctant to give
away precious air time. It is now necessary to court most station
managers and news and public service directors and convince them
that promoting your event will be of value to them and their ratings
as well as in the public interest.

If your cause captures their attention, some will cover the entire
cost, and it can be thousands of dollars, to develop a 15- or 30-sec-
ond public service announcement. Others will air an announcement free if it is produced elsewhere. Explore the possibilities with
your local radio and TV managers. Well-written and produced

PSAs are very effective ways to announce public meetings.

Surveys of newspaper readers have shown that the letters to the editor are second in popularity only to sports. Guest editorials are also widely read. Letters that are brief and state a thoughtful point of view are most likely to be published. That point of view is more credible if it is expressed by a layperson rather than the official in charge. For example, the chair of the citizens' budget committee can urge everyone to come out to the meeting and be involved "in one of the most important fiscal decisions that our town ever has had to make." Offer to ghostwrite a letter or article for a sympathetic citizens' committee or advisory board or to review the facts if they want to write it themselves. Call the paper's editor for rules about length, style, deadlines, and similar matters.

The media release is a common, inexpensive, much-used form of communication. It is somewhat effective if used in combination with other methods, but it should not be relied upon entirely to entice the media to cover your event. Too many releases get trashed because they are addressed to the wrong person, are received too late, are not written succinctly and clearly, or do not portray the sense of importance or urgency the issue deserves.

> *The newly appointed associate director of the local housing agency complained that the agency had not received press coverage for its last five events. "I don't know what to do to get their attention," she complained. "I purposely send out media releases in an unmarked envelope. People are so suspicious of government nowadays that I don't want the editor to prejudge us."*

It is too bad she wastes her time with such misplaced duplicity. The editor or secretary probably throws the envelopes away without opening them just because they are unmarked! Not only should you always use official stationery, but whenever possible enclose a personal note from the company president, the mayor, or another suitable VIP. This will reinforce the importance of the message and help you obtain the attention that your meeting deserves.

How up-to-date is your mailing list of media contacts? Media professionals are especially peripatetic. People move out, on, or up just when they learn the old job. Update your list at least every six months. If you do not have a list, start one. Have a staff person call all your local media—press, radio, and television, including cable—and ask for the names of the people to whom you should address information about your agency. If in doubt about the appropriate recipient, send your release to the editor in chief or city editor of newspapers and the manager or assignment editor of radio and TV stations.

Take special care to spell the name of your recipient correctly. Even if the editor tells you over the phone that his name is John Smith—how straightforward can this be?—ask him how to spell it. He could be a Jon Smythe. Lori or Laurie, Sandi or Sandy, male or female—you get the idea; never take anyone's name for granted.

Always indicate a release date. "For immediate release" is the most common and means that the information can be used when it is received. If needed, be more specific: "For release after 2 p.m. June 5."

Write in the traditional who, what, when, where, and how format still honored by the journalistic profession, but preface your narrative with a headline to get your readers' attention. "Accident at School Crossing Spurs Community Meeting" is more likely to interest the media and the public than the accurate but more mundane, "Community Meeting About Safety to be Held Thursday."

In a brief introductory paragraph, give the bare facts of your meeting. Additional pertinent information (and eye-catching quotes) can be included in subsequent paragraphs. Never write more than one page, double-spaced, although you may include attachments. Conclude with a traditional journalistic ending (####) to show that you know what you're doing.

An "advisory," such as Figure 8.2 on page 105, is a good way to pique the media's interest enough to call you and perhaps even to provide live coverage. Send a short release four or five days before the event, indicating that more information will be available at the meeting. E-mail and the fax machine enable you to send your release without having to rely on the sometimes unpredictable postal service, but you still need to give the media the proper lead time. Always call a day before to remind the people to whom you have written—and do not be dismayed if they say (as most will) that they cannot remember receiving your notice or that they have misplaced it. That is when electronic systems are really handy; you can obligingly send them another immediately. When you speak to them personally, or even if you have to leave a message, apprise them of any special story, photo, or interview opportunity that may be of particular interest to their public.

Figure 8.1 Sample Media Release (should be double-spaced).

City-County Housing Authority
222 Elm Street
Hometown, OR 12345

FOR IMMEDIATE RELEASE
Contact Alice Brown, Assistant Director, 555-1234

Tenant Pet-Denial Policy Subject of Public Meeting

The City-County housing authority will hold a public meeting Wednesday, July 10, at 7 p.m. to evaluate its policy that denies tenants the right to have any pets besides birds and goldfish. The meeting will be held in the agency's auditorium, 222 Elm Street.
The agency is reconsidering its policy after hearing from elderly residents that they would feel less lonely and more secure if they had a dog or a cat as a pet. Other residents say that their small apartments will not accommodate large pets and want a size and weight limit. People with all points of view will be encouraged to speak at the meeting.
"We are open to any suggestions that will increase the feeling of safety and comfort of our tenants without inconveniencing others," said Brenden Block, agency director.

GETTING THE MEDIA TO ANNOUNCE YOUR MEETING

Although there are generalities that apply to dealing with all the media, each facet of this industry is distinct. Though they keep some audio and video tapes, TV and radio are generally more transitory than written articles, which may be read at leisure or clipped for further reference. Yet, even in print—the most permanent of the media—experienced journalists are humbled at least once in their careers by seeing an especially thoughtful piece lining a birdcage or garbage can.

Do not limit your attempts at print coverage to the local general circulation newspaper. In most communities, there are college, high school, and neighborhood papers; church, community, and organizational newsletters; special-interest magazines; and throwaway shoppers—all read by different segments of the public. If you focus on those aspects of your story that are most likely to interest a narrow niche of readers, you will find that smaller presses will give you more space than general circulation newspapers, which have to reach many more competing interests.

Consider, for example, the general media release in Figure 8.1 on

Figure 8.2 Sample Press Advisory.

Tenant Pet-Denial Policy Subject of Public Meeting

The City-County Housing Authority will hold a public meeting Wednesday, July 10, at 7 p.m. to evaluate its policy that denies tenants the right to have any pets besides birds and goldfish. The meeting will be held in the agency's auditorium, 222 Elm Street.

---

page 104, announcing a public meeting to reconsider the pet ownership policy of the local public housing agency. In addition to the general-purpose newspaper, the print media likely to give this story coverage are the senior citizens' weekly, the local veterinary association monthly newsletter, and the neighborhood shopper. The general information—date, time, place—is the same for all. But the angle, or what in the trade is called the "news peg," should vary to suit the audience.

For the senior citizens' newspaper, emphasize that the agency is considering the change in policy in response to requests by some of its elderly residents. Enclose a photo of one or two tenant leaders conferring with the agency director, or suggest where such a photo might be taken. Include quotes from tenants favorable to the openness of the agency in considering their request.

Another approach is necessary to interest the veterinarians in publicizing the meeting. Not unsympathetic to oldsters, they are nevertheless more likely to be interested in how this issue will have an impact on their professional practice and the possibility of obtaining more clients. They might be flattered to be invited to the public meeting as outside experts—an invitation that would also give credence to the agency's claim that it wants to do the right thing.

The news release to the veterinarians' organization should stress the types of animals being considered and note that if the policy is modified, it will be important to make sure that seniors know how to care for their pets. The veterinarians also might be interested in volunteering their services for a monthly pet care clinic or providing ongoing care for residents' pets at reduced fees.

The housing agency also wants to reach the general citizen/taxpayer. The local all-purpose newspaper will probably give the meeting one paragraph buried on the back page, but the shopper, distributed free to every household, is inclined to be more generous with coverage of community events.

The angle that interests the shopper's editor may be neighborhood safety, or perhaps the pros and cons of reconsidering a policy that gives low-income, elderly, and other tenants the same privileges as citizens who live elsewhere. Your release might stress that comments from the entire community are welcome, as evidence that the housing agency realizes its obligation to all citizens. Photos are nearly always welcome, especially if you provide a glossy print. Combine children with seniors and you have a sure winner.

Columnists are another outlet for your story. Every community has at least one who is read and quoted widely. Read the columns over time to get a sense of their style and general content. Most columnists write about human interest—the news behind the news.

In our pet policy example, the veterinarians' donation of time, particularly if one vet is a leading citizen of the community, might be the angle that the local columnist would use. Your release could focus on that, but make sure that the housing agency's public meeting receives appropriate notice too.

Be alert to feature opportunities in other parts of the general-purpose newspaper, for example, letters to the editor and opinion articles discussed earlier. Perhaps there is even the possibility of editorial support. Know your local editor and others who shape the editorial policy of the newspaper well enough that you can call them if there is a crisis and they can call you if they want inside information. This two-way nurturing of open communication and trust will pay off when you need it. You may not always get the editorial approval you want, but you are more likely to be treated fairly and with respect.

Neighborhood and community newspapers are another, often overlooked venue for publicity, especially if you can provide photos. They usually have small staffs—an editor who is also the photographer and one or two inexperienced writers, who will be very appreciative if you suggest an angle that would interest their readers.

The key to dealing successfully with the print media is to realize their variety and segmentation and assign someone to spend the time ferreting out the angles that will get you the greatest coverage with the audience you want most to reach.

If all else fails to garner the publicity you want, pay for it! The decision to buy advertising should not be taken lightly, but neither should it be discarded out of hand. The advantages are twofold: you can choose the medium and you can completely control the message.

> *A regional council of governments in a growing urban area recently sponsored community meetings about the pressing issues of growth and transportation. After failing to interest either of the two daily newspapers in printing articles of any size or depth, the agency produced and paid for its own 12-page, four-color supplement, which was inserted in the Sunday papers. They reached 750,000 people, and the council saw the fruits of its labors and expenditures rewarded. This single, ambitious, expensive effort increased interest and attendance at the public meetings. As a byproduct, the project finally attracted free media attention; reporters realized that these issues did concern a broad range of citizens.*

One of the most important differences between print and the electronic media—television and radio—is the amount of coverage you can reasonably expect. As noted previously, there are many possibilities for stories of some length and depth in the various print media. Generally, however, the most television news coverage that nearly any meeting or public event receives is the few words that fill up 15 or 30 seconds. If you want the important points about your meeting to get across on TV, you need to master the technique of talking in sound bites or headlines.

CONTROL THE INTERVIEW

Answer questions in a short, succinct style. Speak in brief, snappy phrases (10 words or fewer) that convey your basic message. Your ability to communicate well in this medium will pay off when you see your 10-minute interview reduced to a 10-second news headline without significant distortion.

Remembering that television is a visual medium, dress the part whenever you expect or suspect an interview. Your credibility is conveyed by the nonverbal message of how you look before you say anything. When deciding what to wear, consider your audience. What do they expect a person in your position to look like? In the office, you may work comfortably in your shirtsleeves or a simple blouse and skirt; but for a television interview, you convey more authority if you are wearing a jacket. On the other hand, you might want viewers to get the impression that you are a roll-up-your-sleeves, let's-get-to-work kind of person. Your attire must convey an impression of professionalism and competence. Remember, the camera most likely will focus on you from the waist up.

Most people are understandably intimidated by the brash and inquisitorial reporter who pushes a microphone in their face, but there are ways to take control of even that formidable situation.

If reporters corner you at a controversial public meeting, keep cool. Ask them to turn off the camera and mike and give you some idea of the issues they want to cover. Then, request a few minutes to comb your hair, go to the bathroom, and ask a staff person or another public official to join you in the interview. In other words, take whatever time you can to collect your thoughts.

On television, less is more. Wear solid colors in contrasting combinations—dark suit and white or pastel shirt, small-patterned tie for men; suit or dress with simple lines for women. Steer clear of stripes and plaids, loud ties, deep, revealing necklines, and clinky or shiny rings, bracelets, earrings, and cufflinks.

If you are using graphs or charts to explain your point, prepare an extra set, reduced in size, to give the interviewer. It is a good idea to write a short summary of detailed technical information as well, but do not be disappointed if neither is used in the final story.

Establish eye contact with the public by thinking of the camera as representing the vast viewing audience, and looking directly into it—not at the interviewer.

Many people find an interview in the television studio the most difficult media situation of all. You can exercise a modicum of control when interviewed in your own office, on the site, or even at the public meeting you organized; but under the glaring lights and artificial, show-business atmosphere of the TV studio, you may feel totally out of control. All the principles of TV interviewing that we have discussed previously—particularly attention to dress and the ability to speak succinctly—are important in helping you be successful in the studio, but there are others to consider.

The week or day before your interview, watch the program on which you will be interviewed. Familiarize yourself with the format and the set, the style and technique of the hosts. Are they friendly and generally informed? Inquisitorial and probing? Gabby and controlling? Laid-back, letting their guests do most of the talking? Do they seem to have a bias or a particular point of view? What time of day is the program aired? Retired people and women are most likely to watch morning and afternoon TV, while the age and gender of the audience are more varied in the evening. How long is your segment of the program, and what role are you expected to play? Advocate? Resource? Defender of a controversial action or project? Are you being interviewed solo or as part of a panel? Knowing the background before you appear at the studio helps you prepare to give the appropriate responses.

Both men and women look better on television with the addition of some cover-up. A hint of blush adds a healthy glow; facial powder covers perspiring brows and shiny heads, foreheads, and noses. Find out if the studio provides makeup services, and if so, accept them gratefully. If not, whatever your gender, bring along the proper makeup and retire to the restroom beforehand for a touch-up.

At least an hour before, limit your beverage intake to water. Avoid alcohol and caffeine of all kinds, including colas, coffee, and tea. They have a drying effect on what is probably an already tight-with-anticipation throat.

Once the interview begins, ignore the people running around the set with headphones plastered to their ears. They are taking their cues from the director, who is in the sound booth, far removed from the action on the floor.

When you are speaking, do not strain to catch a glimpse of yourself on the nearby monitor. Likewise, avoid trying to figure out which one of the several cameras is focusing on you. The director is making split-second decisions about cameras and all other aspects of the show, so concentrate on your job, which is to look and sound your best.

Pretend that you are in the second grade again and will get marked down for fidgeting, smirking, or looking bored or disgusted, especially when another person is speaking. These spontaneous reactions may be just the ones that the director and camera pick up, to your later dismay.

Understand the importance of body language in reinforcing your image as a credible, trustworthy person. Lean forward to appear friendly and relaxed; sit up straight to emphasize a serious point. Do not smirk, frown, slump, or drape your arm casually over your neighbor's chair. To defuse a hostile or difficult question, smile. Give the viewing audience the impression that you can be trusted.

Do not look furtively around the room or stare at the floor or ceiling; people associate such behavior with deceptiveness.

If you know that you will be seated on the set, will it be behind or around a table or on low couches or chairs? Practice sitting in various positions in front of a mirror at home until you find one that is comfortable and looks good; women should wear a skirt or dress that covers their knees. Keep your feet on the floor and your hands in your lap. This grounding helps you keep control.

If your purpose is to advertise an upcoming public meeting and the host is veering off the subject, be alert for opportunities to get back on track: "I'm glad you brought that up. That's one reason we're eager to hear what the public has to say at our meeting next week." If confronted with an unfair personal attack, state your perspective or position in an affirmative, non-defensive, firm, and honest manner: "I can see where some people would see it that way, but the truth is . . ."

Do not be intimidated by the "pregnant pause"—the interviewer's way of goading you into filling a silence and saying something unexpected. After you have answered a question as completely as you want to, maintain eye contact, smile, take a drink of water, but do not say any more than you intended.

Avoid jargon, acronyms, or technical words that your host and the audience will not understand. Practice the message that you want to convey until it is simple and clear.

When it is all over, watch a tape recording of the program in the comfort of your own living room, alone or with a trusted friend or relative. Be critical. Do you look and sound credible? Is your message clear and succinct? Have you avoided jargon and concepts that are difficult to understand? Are you convincing? Would you be motivated to come to your event or meeting? If you fall short in any area, take this as a cue to improve for your next television opportunity.

Of the three primary media, radio is the most intimate. It is most often background, rather than primary, to your audience of one—rarely more—who is listening while doing something else in the car, bathroom, office, kitchen, or workshop. To capture the listener's attention, train yourself to speak in fragments or 10-word headlines so that whenever listeners tune in, they should be able to get some type of positive message. While the same general rules about the media apply also to radio, there are some special things to consider.

First, there are probably more radio than TV stations in your community. This gives you several choices if you want to reach specific segments of the public. Assign a staff person to find out the focus of each station-news, music (what kind?), talk, national, local, or some mixture—by calling the program manager or a friendly advertising firm that places ads in specific markets. A news or music station with no live segments or interviews might still be induced to read a notice of your public meeting if you send a media release. Know the demographics of each station's listeners and key your release to each. If, for example, the station plays music for the older set, be sure to mention those meeting sites that are particularly accessible. An all-talk radio station, on the other hand, is hungry for guests—especially articulate local people—and would probably welcome your willingness to talk at some length with the host and listening audience about your upcoming public meetings.

Welcome opportunities to be interviewed on talk shows as a way to reach still another segment of the public. As for a television appearance, prepare by listening to the radio program beforehand so that you know the format, the host's general attitude, and the types of questions that may be asked. One important advantage of radio over TV is that the audience cannot see you. You can wear your most comfortable clothes, slump, drape your arm over a chair, even smile, grimace or frown, as long as facial expressions do not affect the quality of your voice, which should be warm and friendly. Present yourself in the same direct, nondefensive way we discussed previously, no matter how opinionated, offensive, or rude the questioner.

Some radio stations will air public service announcements—and even help you record them, if you write the script—even though they are no longer required to do so by the federal government. Develop a friendly relationship with the program manager and you will have a better chance of having your announcement aired during prime listening time rather than at 3 a.m.

If you decide to buy advertising, radio is the least expensive of the mass media.

WHEN THE MEDIA COME TO YOUR MEETING

All the tips that have been provided so far are for one general purpose: to help your agency reach the public through the media and interest them in attending your meeting or event. Well, suppose you are successful; the media *are* interested. They air your announcement, interview you or others, and generally spread the word. The public comes, but so do the media. Now what do you do?

It is very important that one staff person be given responsibility for the care and feeding of the media before, during, and after the meeting, preferably the person who was the principal media contact before the event. At the meeting itself, that job starts with finding and greeting media representatives as they come in the door. Only the TV camera people are obvious; reporters and others look like ordinary folk, especially if they are not carrying note pads. Ask everyone to sign in with name, affiliation, and phone number, and then scan the list for media people you may have missed.

In your pre-meeting planning, decide who will represent the organization and stick to it. If someone else is approached, say something like, "Sorry, I'm not the one to answer that. I'll get Trudy, our manager." Never say, "I'm not authorized to speak to you."

Prepare and hand out a media kit. It should be in a folder and include the release that you sent them (which they may not have read), the agenda of the meeting, background information that will help them report accurately on the event and the names, phone and fax numbers, and e-mail addresses of key contacts. Offer to introduce them to representative VIPs, and be otherwise helpful and accommodating. Most media people guard their hard-boiled personas carefully, and though they rarely say thanks for these courtesies, they nevertheless appreciate and remember them and may reward you by providing accurate and full coverage now and answering your phone calls promptly next time.

Decide in advance where to allow those bulky and intrusive TV cameras to set up. If left to themselves, camera people will choose a spot right in front—the place most convenient for them but distracting to the audience and the presenters. Find a place for the cameras that are as unobtrusive as possible but that still allows for the best camera angles. Remove any audience chairs right behind the cameras before people have claimed them. Television lights are not as blinding as they used to be, and cameras are more quiet. They are tolerated in most courtrooms today and, with the goodwill and cooperation of all parties, can be accommodated at your public meeting.

After the meeting, contact each of the media outlets you notified but did not show up and give them an oral or written summary of the results of the meeting. Though you have controlled as much as you could, one aspect that can get out of control is the audience. One or more people may seek out media attention with untruths or distortions you are not given the opportunity to rebut. Sometimes you just have to live with it. Sometimes the media distort egregiously.

WHEN THE MEDIA ERR

You have done everything to ensure that the media have the right information and are motivated to come to your meeting, and you think that you have given them sufficient tender, loving care to ensure positive results. All they need to do is report the story accurately. How dismaying, then, to hear the evening TV news anchor get it all wrong: "With much reluctance, tonight our city housing agency agreed to let residents have pets, as long as they don't bark or mess on their neighbors' grass. One violation and the pet will be taken away." Another reporter then interviews an elderly resident whom you have never seen before. The resident holds up a little poodle and says, "It's been a long time since I diapered a kid, but the housing people say I have to resort to that with my new puppy."

The next day's newspaper headline reads, "Pet Owners Storm Meeting to Demand Their Rights." Topped by an inflammatory headline, the article, hardly more fair than the TV coverage the night before, quotes concerned residents who commented before the meeting even began, burying in the fourth paragraph information that the meeting was generally amicable, that the vote to allow pets was unanimous, and that no one really "stormed" at or in anything.

If you have followed all the advice in this chapter, such inaccurate reporting is likely to be an infrequent occurrence. Still, if it does happen, you and your staff will be understandably angry and upset. There are several steps you can take, but never consider any of them until after you and everyone else concerned with the issue have had a chance to get the reactions of others more dispassionate. You may find that you are super-sensitive, that most people did not notice what you consider grievous errors. If you still believe that you were injured, you can take several courses of action.

First, analyze the offending reporting objectively. Is it really inaccurate, or is it just another way of stating information? Leaving the question of libel and defamation to the attorneys, you should be concerned with how facts are stated. If you find that the headline is offensive but the story is relatively accurate, do not take any action. Newspaper headline writers are chosen mainly for their speed.

Facing impossible deadlines, they attempt to fit a few descriptive words into a certain space. Generally, editors of neighborhood or community newspapers are responsible for their own headlines, but they, too, are harried and beset with many tasks. Headline writers are allowed to take license to fit the newspaper's layout requirements, and in most cases we have very little leverage to complain—especially if that is the only problem.

The same can be said about the television coverage. In our example, agency representatives did express concern about protecting neighbors against unruly animals, but this was during the introductory part of the meeting. Unfortunately, the TV camera person and reporter left to meet a deadline and were neither briefed by a staff representative about what else was likely to occur nor called later to give them information about what they missed. They had no way of knowing, therefore, that the agency would agree to a public information campaign about responsible pet ownership instead of the fines and removal of offending animals that were first considered. The TV coverage was not in error; it just reported only part of the story. The station would probably welcome a call from you and update the story. This follow-up is likely to result in additional, more positive coverage.

What about the newspaper, radio, or TV editorial that disagrees with your position and proclaims, "The housing agency made an unwise decision last night to allow its tenants to own pets. Low-income people have little enough resources as it is. Now some of them will probably starve themselves to save their animals." The editor or station manager based that opinion on fact; he or she just reached a different conclusion than you would have preferred. It is fruitless to take exception to the media's right to state an opinion. In considering rebuttal, you might suggest that your constituents (not staff) start a letter-writing campaign. You might also try to have your reasons for approving pets given equal time in a guest editorial.

In assessing the extent of wrongdoing, examine all the facts. Was the treatment of the story untrue? Half-true? Or are you just unhappy with the emphasis? Were names or titles misspelled or were comments mistakenly attributed? Does the story damage your reputation or unfairly represent the situation?

If you think you have a legitimate complaint, start your complaining low in the organization. If you know the reporter, call her first: "Phyllis, we really appreciate your covering our meeting on pets yesterday, especially on such a hot night. But I think that you left before we decided on our public information campaign on responsible pet ownership. I'll be glad to get you in touch with the veterinarians who are heading up the program." You have gently chided the reporter but also given her another story—a win/win situation that should always be your goal.

Another approach: "Pete, thanks for the coverage of last night's meeting. But your headline writer seems to have gotten the wrong impression about the attitudes of our tenants." Resist yelling, "Where did your lame-brained headline writer get the idea that people were storming the meeting?" Although you are uncomfortable with the headline, be savvy enough not to hold the reporter responsible. You then can add, "I'd be glad to arrange follow-up interviews with some of our tenants who think that this is the greatest thing since sliced bread." Another win/win.

If you do not know the reporter well, or if you have good reason from prior dealings to distrust her, contact the next-highest person responsible: the editor of that particular department, of the whole newspaper, or the program or station manager. Be sure of your facts and do not rant and rave. People in these positions deal with angry readers/viewers all the time, and they are likely to dismiss you as just another crank unless you present your case reasonably before asking for a retraction or a correction.

Newspapers usually have a space set aside for corrections. If the people you contact disagree with you or refuse to present a correct version, ask the editor if he will accept a letter to the editor or a signed opinion column. It is more difficult to convince TV and radio stations to correct mistakes, though some electronic media do give air time for citizens to express their differences.

In those few cases of absolute misrepresentation, you may need to consult an attorney and take the advice, even if it is to do nothing.

Yes, the media, made up of human beings, do make mistakes: by omission, commission, and sometimes—but more seldom than you may think—by plain meanness and malice.

But do not allow yourself to get upset easily. Choose your battlefield carefully. Work toward a positive, mutual interdependence—you on them to convey the news, and they on you as a news source.

There are times when too much media publicity—"telling and selling" can impede good relations with the public.

A private company was interested in leasing land from the city to build an outdoor amphitheater, primarily for rock concerts. Instead of meeting with nearby residents and businesses to explain the project and talk about how they might mitigate their concerns, they embarked on an extensive media campaign. For two weeks, media carried story after story, accompanied with drawings of the new "state of the art" facility. This widespread publicity enraged rather than engaged the public, and vocal opponents eventually convinced the town council to rescind its prior approval. "They never even talked to us," was the resonating argument from the irate public.

PRINCIPLES OF SUCCESSFUL MEDIA RELATIONS

- All media are not the same. Know the differences and use each to your advantage.
- Honor deadlines. Give the media enough prior notice so that they can schedule someone to cover your event.
- Avoid technical and bureaucratic jargon. The media are your bridge to the public. They cannot convey your message if they do not understand it.
- Be honest. Never be afraid to say, "I don't know," but always add, "I'll find out for you."
- Make yourself or others in your agency or organization available for background information or interviews.
- Remember that one picture is worth a thousand words, but you may have to stage that photo opportunity yourself, or have your staff prepare clear graphics.
- Write clearly and succinctly, following the who-what-when-where-how formula.
- Submit written materials double-spaced, with all names, dates, and places double-checked for accuracy.
- Prepare media kits to distribute to reporters who come to your meeting, and to those who stay away.
- Look for less obvious publicity niches to reach segments of the public that are important to notify of the meeting.
- Know your local editors and station or program managers, and be a reliable news source.
- Dress appropriately when the camera is on or might be.

- Face the inevitable—bad news does indeed drive out good news—but take that as a challenge to convince the media otherwise.
- Be friendly with the media, but do not expect the media to be your friends. Everyone has a job to do, and the public is best served if each one does it well.

9

Step-By-Step Checklist For Meeting Planners

If there is one point you should always remember about organizing public meetings, it is never to leave anything to chance—or the last minute. This checklist, divided into pre-meeting, meeting, and post-meeting phases, should help you cover everything. It assumes you are planning a public meeting for 50 to 100. The same steps are needed for a smaller or larger group, though, of course, the exact details and amount of staff and other resources will differ.

PRE-MEETING

1. Set aside sufficient time and resources for planning. Two months or six weeks ahead is not too soon, especially if the desired space is popular and must be reserved well in advance or if there are several presenters and audiovisuals that need to be coordinated.

2. Top management should indicate the importance of the event by attending key planning meetings: at the beginning, when the goals and objectives, format, and presenters are chosen; in the middle, before final decisions are made; and the one or more rehearsals.

3. Appoint a staff committee with a chair or manager responsible for overseeing the entire event. Include on that committee graphics or audiovisual preparers; at least one secretary or clerical assistant to take minutes and keep lists of tasks and responsibilities; perhaps someone from another department or a friendly citizen who may have special knowledge of the subject, of the audience, or of controversial issues that should be covered; and all presenters. Experts or outside consultants should be encouraged to attend as many meet-

ings as possible. This core group should work together throughout the entire planning and execution phases.

4. Assign someone to be in charge of media relations for this event. If your organization has a public information office with several employees, the media for this meeting should be the responsibility of one individual. It is to your advantage to begin early to develop ideas for special coverage and to cultivate those media representatives who may be particularly receptive.

5. Make assignments for all other specific roles: drivers and vans to transport bulky equipment, registrars, people to post signs, and a general gofer.

6. At your first get-together, agree on the basic purpose of the meeting: informational, advisory, or problem-solving, and your desired outcome. Design the format to help you reach your goals and objectives. Never promise more to the public than you are willing or able to deliver. For example, do not set up a problem-solving meeting when you have no intention of changing your plan or project in response to suggestions that citizens might have. It is more credible and acceptable to tell the audience that the meeting is purely informational.

7. Notify the potential audience as early as possible, if only with a brief notice, "Save this date for an important meeting. More later."

8. In deciding the length of the meeting, always keep in mind the likely expectations and endurance of the audience. The productivity of most public meetings decreases after two or two and one-half hours as attendees become restless and inattentive. It should be added that the endurance level of the organizers is similarly affected, though they are less able to show it. If the meeting is to last a whole or half-day, plan to allow breaks periodically. Generally, evening meetings should end before 10 o'clock. Rather than wearing out everyone, end on a high note, even if you have to agree to have another meeting to continue the exciting discussion.

9. Decide early in the planning the best place to hold the meeting, for the convenience of the participants, not yourselves. Have a back-up if the first choice is unavailable. Assign someone to visit the site to make certain that it meets your requirements.

10. List everything that needs to get done and agree on responsibilities and deadlines. Distribute the schedule to everyone involved and update as needed.

11. Make a floor plan of the meeting room, placing the tables and

chairs, graphics, and other accessories. Locate electrical outlets and ascertain if you are allowed to tack materials to the walls. This eases the panic of having to make major decisions at the last minute, though a certain flexibility is necessary to meet unexpected situations.

12. Identify the name and phone number of the caretaker or janitor and make sure he has the floor plan and will be available if you need help with extra chairs and tables or any other needs.

> *The meeting planners were pleased they had the use of the media center in this small rural school. It was just the size and location to attract the farmers they wanted to attend to talk about issues important to their livelihoods. The organizers came early to set up their chairs and tables, having received the key to the locked storage cabinet the day before. But to their dismay, they found the restrooms locked, too, and they had no key for those vital facilities. No one had the principal's unlisted home number and there was no way to reach the custodian. "We'll have a riot on our hands if we can't use the restrooms," moaned the project manager, as he authorized an employee to pry loose the unsubstantial lock. The next day, they apologized to the principal and sent a locksmith to repair the damage.*

13. Meet regularly to review roles and responsibilities, report on progress, and make adjustments to the schedule when necessary. As noted previously, the department or agency manager does not need to attend all these meetings but should send a representative and be alerted to any major problems that arise.

14. Begin to develop concepts for graphics as soon as the subject of the various presentations is decided. Write and review an outline of any slide show or video; then, write and review the script. Finally, before production, prepare and review a "story board" or photo/script outline. If several levels of content review are required, build them into your schedule.

15. Review drafts of all oral presentations, maps, and charts to make sure that they are unambiguous, consistent, clear, and concise. Hold this review sufficiently ahead of the meeting that appropriate changes can be made.

16. Develop or refine your mailing list. Who must be notified to comply with legal or regulatory requirements? Who should be notified to show your goodwill and openness? Design your mailings carefully according to criteria discussed in Chapter 3. If you have no legal requirements for timing, notification by U.S. mail or e-mail 10 days or two weeks ahead is adequate. Do not notify people too much in advance or they will forget. If you can afford two mailings, send the first three weeks ahead and the follow-up within a week of the meeting.

17. Make a list of those who should receive special notes or reminder calls and assign someone to take care of that. VIPs may require a personal telephone call or a letter from the manager or high-prestige official. Your VIP list may include leaders of key organizations, political or community influentials, and important personnel within your or other agencies.

18. Order the refreshments, taking into account your budget and the expectations and preferences of your audience. Always have something, if only tea and coffee.

19. Prepare a complete inventory of all needed materials and equipment and test to make sure that everything is in working order.

20. Stock a meeting kit that contains at least the following: small and large pads, pens, pencils, scissors, marking pens, chalk, name tags, extra projector bulbs, portable phone, extension cords, aspirin, clear tape, masking tape, and duct tape.

21. About a week before the meeting, hold a dry run in your office to review everything that will be said and done. Include the people who participated in your early planning sessions but have not been involved in subsequent day-to-day activities. If at all possible, rehearse with the outside presenters. At the least, have an advance copy of their remarks and check for ambiguities, repetition, and inconsistencies. Make notes of any changes that you agree upon and make sure that they are made.

22. To assure uniformity and quality control, write a guide for discussion leaders and recorders that includes the issues that they should cover and general rules for chairing a discussion. Hold a training session before the meeting to review what is expected.

23. Write a short questionnaire to be completed by participants before they leave. Include queries about issues as well as those that evaluate the quality of the meeting.

24. A day ahead (or a few hours, if you cannot get everyone

together or the room is unavailable), hold a dress rehearsal on the site. This will do much to allay your fears and stage fright and will reveal the inevitable problems—charts that need bigger titles in order to be read, awkward positioning for the projector and screen, electrical outlets that do not work, and other unforeseen glitches— enough in advance that you can do something about them.

25. Set aside time to go over the ground rules and agenda with all discussion leaders and recorders. An hour before the meeting should be sufficient.

26. Arrive early to arrange everything according to plan. Put up the directional signs first. There are always people who come early!

DURING THE MEETING

1. After you have double-checked to be sure everything is in place, start at the appointed time. If all your planning has been sufficient and you have taken care of everything noted in this book, you should be on your way to a successful session that satisfies you and your audience.

2. Make sure the troubleshooter is poised to take care of the inevitable last-minute problems, and has a phone and emergency numbers.

3. Assign one or more people to staff the registration table at least through the halfway mark to meet and greet latecomers and orient them to what is being taken up on the program at that time.

4. End on time. Honor the agreement you made with all the participants, but offer to stay later to accommodate anyone who has additional questions.

POST-MEETING

1. At the beginning of the planning process, when you make up your schedule, set a time for recap and evaluation as soon as possible, but no later than a week afterward. Invite everyone who participated in the planning and execution. For more dispassionate opinions, you may also want to include interested outsiders.

2. The meeting should be chaired by the department or agency manager and invite a candid discussion of everything that occurred. The original outline of purpose and goals should provide the benchmark. Did the meeting reach or exceed the expectations you set previously? What did you all learn that will help you carry out the project or program? What was the reaction of the public? Are other

meetings necessary? Should you schedule additional follow-up, such as letters or telephone calls, to specific groups or individuals? Was the media coverage adequate or what you expected? If there were any problems with the media, how should they be handled? What worked particularly well? What should be improved upon next time?

3. Choose individuals to carry out post-meeting activities, such as reporting on and distributing a summary of the meeting to participants, the media, key community activists, or decision makers, and writing thank-you notes to any particularly helpful individuals.

4. As a guide for the future, assign someone to write an evaluation of the meeting. File it in an accessible place with copies of all pertinent file materials.

5. Give praise where warranted. There should be enough to go around.

10

Final Thoughts

Intimidated? Frustrated? Excited? Challenged? By now, you may feel these emotions, and more, after realizing all the aspects of public meetings that have to be considered before you declare success. Take heart; as we hope this book attests, you can do it, and even one victory can spur you and your colleagues on to even greater heights. If you still have unanswered questions, the following may help.

Question: Even the most well-organized format can be disrupted by a company CEO or agency official who takes over and talks too much. Can this can be controlled without losing our jobs?

Answer: The best way to handle this unfortunate situation is to anticipate it. When planning the meeting, contact your organization's high-ranking people or their representatives, review the agenda and the reasons behind it, and offer to give the VIP a few minutes for general greetings. Emphasize the tight schedule and the importance of getting on with the purpose of the meeting as quickly as possible. Most reasonable people will comply. If the VIP arrives at the meeting unannounced, expecting to be heard at any length, be as assertive as you can. Start the meeting on time by graciously telling the audience that "we have an unexpected guest" who "wants to say a few words." You may need to reaffirm the agenda for all to hear: "As we can all see, we have many items to cover in a very short time." This will shame most pushy executives into behaving. The few who insist on talking too much will lose more credibility with the audience than you will.

Question: Understanding the risks in giving into disrupters by adjourning a meeting early and thus making it appear they have achieved their goal, are there any times this is acceptable?

Answer: Generally, as noted in Chapter 7, when it appears matters may get out of control, it is better to take a short recess and reorganize than to adjourn the meeting precipitously. In my 25 years experience, the only time I took the latter step was when thugs brought guns to a crowded meeting in the small community's only school and slouched silently around the room in a decidedly threatening manner. I tried to ignore them and go on with the agenda as one of my assistants sneaked outside to call the sheriff on a cell phone. When the authorities arrived and advised us to adjourn while they took care of the troublemakers, most of the people in the audience filed out quietly. Some thanked us for taking care of the matter in this way. Even so, a few community leaders in this rural area reproached me for the "unnecessary" action. "They're our guys and we could have handled them if they got out of line," they said. In a similar situation in another community where there was only one disrupter, the police were called and quietly removed the agitator, allowing us to continue our meeting.

Question: How can we know when our written notices work? Do the same rules apply when we are trying to reach 100, 1,000, or 100,000 people?

Answer: The surest sign that your written notices are effective is when the approximate number and kind of people that you expected show up at the meeting. There often are surprises: a smaller or greater number or different people than you thought would be interested. In the latter case, the word was probably distributed by one or more special interests—people who found out about the meeting and took the responsibility to make sure their colleagues knew about it. That also may account for the increased numbers.

If fewer people come than anticipated, the notice may have been adequate, but the day or location inconvenient, or else not very many people are interested in the issue. Chapter 4 contains suggestions about how to handle unexpectedly low or high numbers.

Generally, however, the same rules apply about notices, no matter the number to whom they are sent. They all should be clear, concise, and inviting. The techniques vary, of course. You are not likely to be able to afford to send individual notices to 100,000 people, especially if you are notifying them of a series of meetings, not just one. In that case, paid media advertising and public service announcements are effective techniques. The fewer the number of invitees, the more you can target or segment the notice so that it reaches your precise audiences. Do not neglect translating English into other languages if that is required to catch the attention of certain groups.

Question: In graphics, are there any colors that should be avoided?

Answer: Yes. Do not use light yellows or pastels, unless they are on a very strong, dark background. Bold colors, blue, dark green, red, black, and brown are preferred—they are clear and can be seen most readily at a distance. If you are using colors as symbols, choose those that are easily recognizable by the audience. For example, some very effective transportation-related displays use red to show unacceptable (stop) options, yellow (caution) for neutral, and green (go) for those most people favor. When coloring a map, blue should be reserved for water, green for trees, and brown or a neutral tone for land. Resist trendy or decorator colors that may be all the rage in interior decorating, only to go out of fashion quickly.

Question: Why is it so important to start and end on time?

Answer: For the simple reason that your audience has the right to expect that you will use their time wisely, beginning and ending on time is the best proof. If everyone is given an agenda with the approximate schedule, time can be your ally in keeping control and on track. You can offer to stay later for the few who want to prolong the discussion, but most participants—audience and presenters—will appreciate a firm cutoff time.

Question: This book has not even mentioned Robert's Rules of Order or other systems. Shouldn't any routine procedures be used?

Answer: Robert's, Roberto's, Roberta's, whatever, it is important that any procedures you follow do not stifle creative and worthwhile discussion. Knowing when and how to make motions, second them, move for reconsideration, etc. are necessary for rule-making bodies but impediments to informational or problem-solving public meetings. You should always follow general rules of behavior, however, stressing courtesy and civility. These certainly should be enforced by the chair or facilitator.

Question: What are effective feedback techniques to make sure people really understand the issues?

Answer: The question and answer session following the presentations should give meeting organizers a good clue about whether people understand what was said and their level of agreement. Asking participants to complete a short questionnaire evaluating the meeting itself as well as giving room for comments about the issues discussed is another valuable feedback technique. Remember, though, that they may understand the issues thoroughly and still reserve the right to disagree with your solutions!

Another way to gauge public reaction is to keep track of how many e-mails, faxes, telephone calls, or letters to the editor the meeting elicited. Or ask some people who were there to give you frank opinions. Use whatever formal and informal avenues you have to determine the level of understanding and acceptance that resulted from the meeting and be prepared to take the appropriate action.

Question: Many communities routinely broadcast local public meetings over cable access television. How important is this?

Answer: The smaller the population, the greater the likelihood that citizens tune into their local cable access channel to see what is happening down at city hall or the county courthouse. This is an inexpensive and expedient way to broadcast the unrehearsed activities of elected and appointed officials, boards, and commissions. If the cable folks come to your meeting, welcome them warmly and find an unobtrusive place for their camera. They usually do not edit the broadcasts, and your meeting will be so well organized and presented that you will be proud to have people view it from the comfort of their living rooms.

Question: What are the differences between public information and public involvement and how do they affect the kind of public meeting we plan?

Answer: As stated several times in this book, one of the first matters to decide before organizing your public meeting is what is its primary purpose: informational, advisory, or problem-solving. The first type is by and large one-way—presenters tell the audience what they want them to hear, with minimum involvement invited. The latter two should have built-in techniques, not only for providing information but also for involving the public in discussing possible solutions. You cannot expect this to happen unless you create the best environment and use the appropriate public involvement techniques.

Question: Everyone is busy. What is the minimum amount of time that should be spent to ensure a successful public meeting?

Answer: This depends on many factors. Certainly, consider the complexity of the meeting format, number of people expected, and the number of staff that can be deployed for planning and execution. Start about six weeks ahead of time and hold at least one two- to three-hour planning meeting each subsequent week. Of course, this does not count the time spent in between meetings actually carrying out all the tasks. At your evaluation meeting afterwards, include a discussion of how much time was actually spent by all and a frank assessment of whether it was too much (probably not), too little (more than likely), or just enough (you hope).

Question: How can you get a community or group of people to come to a meeting about a subject that is important but noncontroversial?

Answer: First of all, do you really have to have that meeting? Perhaps there are more effective ways to get the word out and involve people, such as giving presentations to specific groups that appear to be interested rather than expecting them to come to a meeting you organize. If you want to spur people to act, consider sponsoring an event, such as a tree planting or neighborhood clean-up. These are more successful when held in partnership with recognized groups who can spread the word to their own members. In other words, public meetings are only one way to communicate with people, and they may not always be the best way.

Question: Can a good web site take the place of a public meeting? What about videoconferencing?

Answer: Some people will pay attention to a "virtual meeting" on the Internet when they will never leave their doorsteps to come out to a public meeting. Refer to Chapter 6 for guidance about how to build and maintain web sites that capture attention and stimulate productive comments. But remember that many others do not have daily access to the technology.

Videoconferences—giving people the opportunity to interact with each other from different locations—are expensive and should be considered only if you have the budget to do it well, this is the only way to bring these people together, and they and the subject will benefit from this interaction. The fact that they are "on camera" and in a somewhat formal and constrained environment intimidates some people from talking freely and may encourage others to talk too much.

Consider both the web site and videoconference as other ways to contact people and obtain feedback, while making sure you do not neglect at least trying to get them in the same room face to face in vigorous and healthy discourse.

Question: This whole book is devoted to "public meetings." Yet, most of us spend more of our time in small staff meetings. Are there any transferable techniques?

Answer: Naturally, there are many differences, but the same general principles should apply:

- Plan ahead, with an agenda that meets the goals of the meeting and the time allowed
- Always start and end on time
- Choose an environment conducive to frank and open discussion
- Be an informed facilitator or presenter sensitive to the needs of your listeners
- Use graphics that are clear, concise, and unambiguous
- Have a feedback system that accurately gauges the opinions and concerns of the participants
- Celebrate your successes and learn from your failures
- Have fun!

Index